Year of the Yankees

Year of the Yankees

Lou Sahadi

Contemporary Books, Inc.
Chicago

Library of Congress Cataloging in Publication Data

Sahadi, Lou.
    Year of the Yankees.

    Includes index.
    1. New York.   2. Baseball club (American League)
I. Title.
GV875.N4S23   1979   796.357'64'097471   79-50039
ISBN 0-8092-7212-1

**Black-and-white photos: New York Yankees,
World Wide Photos, and Mickey Palmer**

**Color photos: Mickey Palmer,
"Focus on Sports"**

Published by Contemporary Books, Inc.
180 North Michigan Avenue, Chicago, Illinois 60601
Manufactured in the United States of America
Library of Congress Catalog Card Number: 79-50039
International Standard Book Number: 0-8092-7212-1

Published simultaneously in Canada by
Beaverbooks
953 Dillingham Road
Pickering, Ontario L1W 1Z7
Canada

For Jack who had an idea;
Stu who had no idea;
and to David and John who inspired the idea.

Contents

Acknowledgments

The author would like to express his thanks to Mickey Morabito and Larry Wahl of the New York Yankees for their assistance in gathering material for this book.

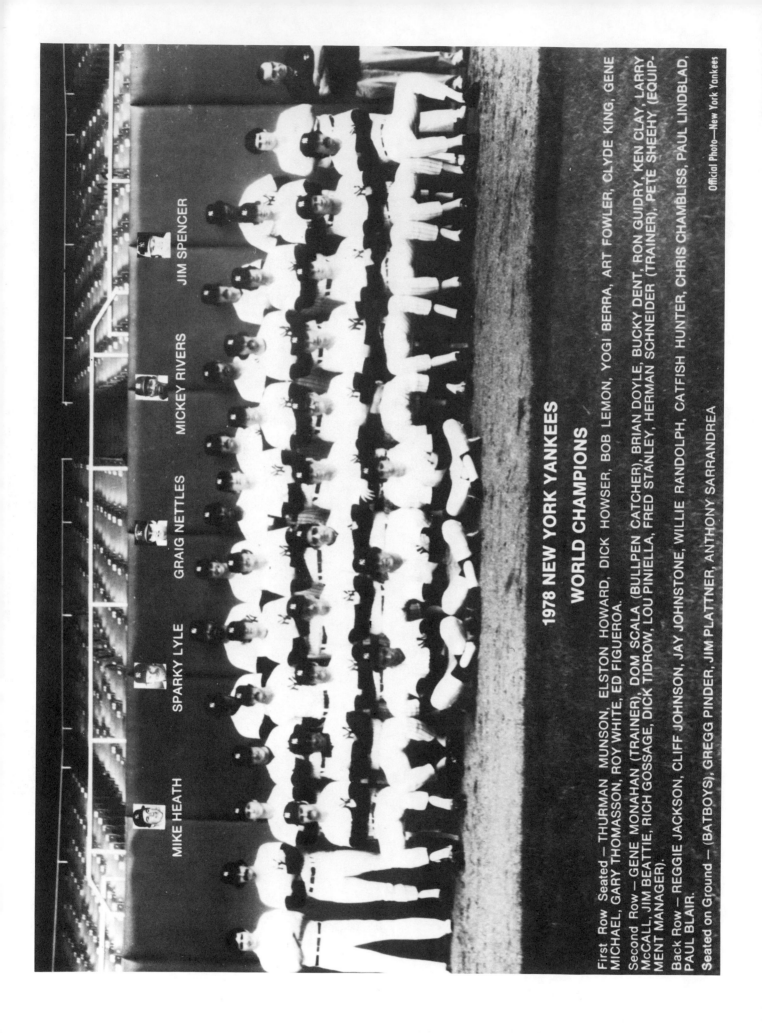

MIKE HEATH   SPARKY LYLE   GRAIG NETTLES   MICKEY RIVERS   JIM SPENCER

1978 NEW YORK YANKEES

WORLD CHAMPIONS

First Row Seated — THURMAN MUNSON, ELSTON HOWARD, DICK HOWSER, BOB LEMON, YOGI BERRA, ART FOWLER, CLYDE KING, GENE MICHAEL, GARY THOMASSON, ROY WHITE, ED FIGUEROA.

Second Row — GENE MONAHAN (TRAINER), DOM SCALA (BULLPEN CATCHER), BRIAN DOYLE, BUCKY DENT, RON GUIDRY, KEN CLAY, LARRY McCALL, JIM BEATTIE, RICH GOSSAGE, DICK TIDROW, LOU PINIELLA, FRED STANLEY, HERMAN SCHNEIDER (TRAINER), PETE SHEEHY (EQUIPMENT MANAGER).

Back Row — REGGIE JACKSON, CLIFF JOHNSON, JAY JOHNSTONE, WILLIE RANDOLPH, CATFISH HUNTER, CHRIS CHAMBLISS, PAUL LINDBLAD, PAUL BLAIR.

Seated on Ground — (BATBOYS), GREGG PINDER, JIM PLATTNER, ANTHONY SARRANDREA

GEORGE M. STEINBRENNER
Principal Owner

AL ROSEN
President

CEDRIC TALLIS
V.P., General Manager

BOB LEMON
Manager

YOGI BERRA
Coach

ART FOWLER
Coach

ELSTON HOWARD
Coach

DICK HOWSER
Coach

GENE MICHAEL
Coach

DELL ALSTON
Outfielder

JIM BEATTIE
Pitcher

PAUL BLAIR
Outfielder

CHRIS CHAMBLISS
First Baseman

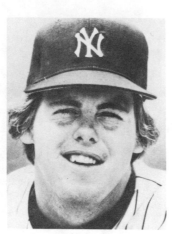

KEN CLAY
Pitcher

BUCKY DENT
Shortstop

RAWLY EASTWICK
Pitcher

WILLIE RANDOLPH
Second Baseman

MICKEY RIVERS
Outfielder

JIM SPENCER
1B - OF

FRED STANLEY
Infielder

DICK TIDROW
Pitcher

ROY WHITE
Outfielder

GARY THOMASSON
Outfielder

DAMASO GARCIA
Infielder

CLIFF JOHNSON
C - 1B - OF

LARRY McCALL
Pitcher

SPARKY LYLE
Pitcher

ANDY MESSERSMITH
Pitcher

THURMAN MUNSON
Catcher

GRAIG NETTLES
Third Baseman

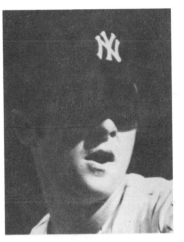

BOB KAMMEYER
Pitcher

LOU PINIELLA
Outfielder

ED FIGUEROA
Pitcher

RICH GOSSAGE
Pitcher

RON GUIDRY
Pitcher

DON GULLETT
Pitcher

MIKE HEATH
Catcher

JAY JOHNSTONE
Outfielder

JIM "CATFISH" HUNTER
Pitcher

REGGIE JACKSON
Outfielder

1
George Steinbrenner

He is often misunderstood. Otherwise, why would he be considered so controversial? It's just that those around him really don't understand him. All will agree that he is a perfectionist. This is at the root of his psyche. He can be a rough taskmaster, whether engaged in business or in baseball. He demands perfection and very often achieves it. Simply, he is a model of success and he wants others to emulate his accomplishments. He leads by example. Second best is not acceptable. The bottom line is winning. Anything short of that goal is unsuccessful. That's the way that George Steinbrenner thinks and operates. And he doesn't disguise it, either.

He is a driven man. He can be charming one moment and explosive the next. Players as well as front office personnel have felt his anger. Even writers covering the club are leery of him. Yet, in many ways Steinbrenner is a sensitive person. Nothing angers him more than a story that has been inaccurately reported. It is all part of his makeup, one that

offers no excuses in the pursuit of excellence. And through it all, he admits that he is a difficult person to understand fully.

"I know I'm tough," confessed Steinbrenner. "But I try to make up to my people in other ways. I don't like to hurt people. Sometimes I just, well, I can't help it. I'm the heavy. I don't like it, but I don't know how to change it. No one has been able to capture the real me, how I feel. I guess it's tough. It's hard for me to convey what I really feel. It's not something that I can easily say.

"I've always kept my emotions inside me. They tell me I don't let myself go, and that's true. It's a mark of strength among Germans, you know. It isn't that frequent that I really enjoy myself. It's hard to explain, but the feeling I got after winning a World Series wasn't what I thought it would be. I remember saying to myself, 'I wonder why I'm not more excited?' But then I saw the happiness I got was seeing happiness in others.

"It's like when a cab driver comes up to

1

me and says, 'Thanks for bringing the Yankees back.' Even if it's just 'Thanks for spending your money,' it's unreal. I feel so good about winning one for New York. This is the greatest city in the world, and its people are the greatest people in the world. And I just hope they like me."

Like him or not, one has to admire Steinbrenner. One has to respect the plateau of excellence he has achieved for the Yankees ever since the day in 1973 he purchased them with a group of other investors. The once mighty Yankees had fallen on lean times. The dynasty that had dominated baseball had crumbled. Not only were the Yankees not winning on the field, but they were losing at the box office, too. The city's baseball minions had switched their allegiance to the New York Mets. Imagine an expansion team in a sophisticated city like New York overshadowing the once proud and powerful Yankees!

It bothered Steinbrenner. As an empire builder himself in the shipbuilding business, he couldn't justify the way a baseball dynasty like the Yankees had come apart. Even as a child growing up in Cleveland, the now 48-year-old Steinbrenner had a respect for the Yankees during their years of glory. While others condemned their success, he admired it. Now, in 1973, he stood among the ruins, determined to restore the grandeur of the Yankees. It was an obsession with him, a private war. It was a war that he didn't intend to lose. One could see a bit of General Patton in him.

Like Patton, Steinbrenner had relentless drive and ambition, which was exactly what the Yankees needed. Owned by CBS at the time, certainly the team was already invested with wealth and power. The one ingredient they lacked was a leader. It was as if Steinbrenner had been born for the role. Deep down he relished the challenge. He began to take the necessary steps to assume the role. At the time of the purchase from CBS, Steinbrenner owned 20 percent of the Yankees. Quietly, he began to buy out his partners in the original deal. Steinbrenner now owns 55 percent of the club, which allows him latitude to operate.

Besides wealth and determination, Steinbrenner also had vision. His personal goal was to make the Yankees world champions in five years. At the time, some felt he was too ambitious. But the more Steinbrenner faced the challenge, the more his drive intensified. His private war became known. The baseball world was aware that Steinbrenner was indefatigable in his objective. In four years, the Yankees became champions of the American League. They were almost there. In 1977 the Yanks completed Steinbrenner's quest. Steinbrenner was satisfied that the Yankees were the champions of the world. He came into a bleak setting with his eyes wide open and made it rosy the only way he knew how, by winning it all.

"When I came here five years ago, all you ever heard about were the Mets," remarked outfielder Lou Piniella. "Now all you ever hear is the Yankees. That's George."

Yet, it hasn't been easy for Steinbrenner. Only a person with his tenacity could have endured the pain and anguish that has enveloped his reign as emperor of the Yankees. In the first six years in which he has ruled the Yankees, Steinbrenner has employed three different managers. Very few remember that Bill Virdon was the first manager to work for Steinbrenner. They forget simply because of the tumultuous years of Billy Martin, Virdon's successor in 1975. If there is one single regret Steinbrenner has had over the years it is the strained relationship he has had with the stormy Martin.

There is no question that Steinbrenner admires Martin's forte as a manager. If he didn't, he wouldn't have hired him to manage the Yankees midway into the 1975 season. He was Steinbrenner's hand-picked choice. A gutsy street fighter, Martin always played to win, even when he was an infielder with the Yankees. His dedication to winning didn't go unnoticed by Steinbrenner. And Martin won in 1976 and 1977 before a deterioration in the overall atmosphere surrounding the club forced him to resign his post halfway through the 1978 season. It was undoubtedly the low point in the surge of success that Steinbrenner had restored to the Yankees.

Yet, the two had a deep relationship. Each did respect the other's contributions. It was as if Steinbrenner saw in Martin the type of manager he would have been if he had ever dreamed of being one. In the three years they were together, there were numerous arguments and disagreements. But each had the same purpose and that was to win. Prophetically, they made a beer commercial together—the punch line at the end showing Steinbrenner firing Martin. Steinbrenner only wished that it never happened in real life. Unfortunately, it did.

"We have never worked better together than we have the last two or three weeks," admitted Steinbrenner the night Martin quit. "I was shocked on learning of his remarks in Chicago. You could have knocked me over. The events that have transpired in the last hours have little significance when compared to a man's concern for his own well-being. These things, along with his family, are far more important than the game of baseball.

"I am grateful to Billy for his contributions as manager of the Yankees. He brought us a championship. His apologies over the recent incident are accepted with no further comment necessary. I think Billy knows of our concern for the well-being of his family and himself. We wish him good luck."

Martin's stormy exit as manager of the Yankees shocked the baseball world. He had cracked under the pressure of his job at a time during the 1978 season when things were not going well on the field. Yet, only a week later, on Old Timer's Day, an annual Yankee tradition, Steinbrenner brought Martin back. He not only brought Martin back for that day, but he also announced that Martin would return as field manager of the Yankees in 1980.

Steinbrenner had the instinct to keep in touch with the real world. During the week following Martin's resignation, the Yankee offices were deluged with telephone calls and letters supporting the popular manager. With a flair for theatrics. Steinbrenner quickly moved to bring Martin back before a sold-out crowd in Yankee Stadium. Not even any of the other Yankee players knew what Steinbrenner had accomplished. It was perhaps the most popular maneuver Steinbrenner ever made in his six years as head of the Yankees.

And yet, Steinbrenner almost always seems to be in the eye of the storm. He is known to have admonished certain players behind closed doors of the Yankee clubhouse. Every so often he has had disagreements with such star players as Thurman Munson, Reggie Jackson, and Sparky Lyle. Yet, he appears to enjoy the role of catalyst, of father image to his players. Perhaps it is his way of showing he wants to belong. Despite his power and wealth, he retains a feeling of being one of the boys, which is hard for a person of Steinbrenner's stature. Yet, in his own way, he tries. Perhaps he tries too hard.

What really excites him is someone coming up to him on the street and shaking his hand, telling him how much he appreciates what he has done for the Yankees. It gives him a feeling of being needed and recognized for what he has done in a small sort of way. Quite possibly, he enjoys this closeness more than all the dinners and the platitudes that go with them.

"Class, what class they have," says Steinbrenner about the little guy on the street. "I wish I had class like that. I wish I had the class to go up to a stranger and thank him for something. I don't."

"It's simple. Yet, for someone like Steinbrenner, it is difficult. It could possibly be attributed to his strict upbringing by a German father and an Irish mother. His father was a tough disciplinarian and successful businessman who owned his own shipping company. He was grooming his son to take over his business one day and insisted that he learn at a young age to work and work harder than anyone else who worked for him. He provided his son with a rigid military school background as the basis for higher formal education. It worked. Today, Steinbrenner is chairman of the board of the American Ship Building Company and owns a hotel, thoroughbred farm, and real estate holdings on Florida's west coast, plus Kinsman Shipping, which he bought from his father, and various banking and land investments.

Being involved in so many enterprises gives him little time to relax. The Yankees offer him that platform, at least when there isn't any turmoil such as spring training which ushers in a new season and a new beginning. In 1977 there was such turmoil, but no signs of it appeared in 1978 at the Yankee's base in Ft. Lauderdale. One day Steinbrenner sat in the Yankee dugout, watching his players and trying to be one of the boys, so to speak. At that moment, Piniella caught his attention.

"Lou," yelled Steinbrenner, "that hat is too small."

"I need some sun, George," answered Piniella about his ridiculously small hat.

"Oh, you Spaniards all tan quick," shot back Steinbrenner.

It was obvious that Steinbrenner was relaxed. He sat among his players and was looking forward to the 1978 season. He felt confident that his club would repeat as world champions, having made several off-season deals that strengthened the team. One was the acquisition of baseball's top relief pitcher Rich Gossage in the free agent market. Another was signing Cincinnati's top reliever Rawly Eastwick the same way.

"Things are going just great," exclaimed Steinbrenner. "Sure, we have problems, but every team has problems. The thing is that this year it will be so much easier. The players understand each other, and they understand what Billy and I want. They went through hell last year, but they all were toughened by the experience."

Steinbrenner himself was a strong focal point of that experience. Besides his clubhouse dissertations, more than once he had to go one-on-one privately with some of his key players, notably Munson, Lyle, and Jackson, often the result of misunderstandings or incidents blown out of proportion by writers.

The bitter feelings Munson harbored for Jackson were a result of contract squabbling. Munson claimed that Steinbrenner told him he would be the most highly paid Yankee except for Catfish Hunter. When Jackson's total contract was made known, Munson rebelled. He felt he had been misled and demanded to be traded. Jackson did not receive more money than Munson on an annual basis but generally more in deferred payments. Munson remained bitter and wanted to quit.

"You really didn't think he'd quit," remarked Steinbrenner. "It was just a misunderstanding. Misunderstandings happen in business."

When Steinbrenner signed Gossage, Lyle was infuriated. Lyle had won the Cy Young Award in 1977 as the best pitcher in the American League. Now, Lyle anticipated he would be playing a lesser role and Gossage would be the team's bullpen ace. He, too, demanded to be traded. But Steinbrenner kept him.

"Like I told Sparky, 'How much market value is there for a 34-year-old reliever?'" snapped Steinbrenner.

The owner made his point. Lyle fumed in the bullpen all season long as Gossage was the talk of the league. When the 1978 season ended, Lyle got his wish. He was traded to the Texas Rangers in a multiple-player deal.

Yet, Steinbrenner is a generous owner. He pays his players well. It is distinctly possible that the Yankees have the largest payroll in baseball. He is addicted to the star system, not only because of productivity on the field, but because of ticket appeal as well. As such, the Yankees are the biggest draw in the major leagues. He gives his players first class treatment, tossing them bonuses and taking care of their bills in certain hotels and restaurants. At times he has given gifts to the players' wives.

"Steinbrenner is a man of his word," claims Hunter. "Even though a lot of times you have to get it in writing to make sure of it."

One thing is sure: If Steinbrenner is upset

by the performance of the team, he lets each and every one know about it in no uncertain terms. Whether his clubhouse speeches are effective can't be determined. But at least he does make his point and feelings known.

"Once you've heard the first one or two, you can almost sleep through the others," admits Hunter. "He means well, but they always sound the same. It's always how we're embarrassing ourselves and embarrassing New York and baseball and the country."

One item that Steinbrenner will not be embarrassed by is the quality of the players on his payroll. Over the last few years he has spent more money on free agent players than any other owner in baseball. If Steinbrenner had an opportunity to strengthen the Yankees, he wouldn't miss it. His free agent acquisitions read like an All-Star team, with the emphasis on pitching. They included Jackson, Hunter, Gossage, Eastwick, Don Gullett, and for 1979, Tommy John and Luis Tiant. The cost of the entire package is about $13.5 million.

"I don't like free agency," disclosed Steinbrenner. "I never did like it. I didn't create it, and I promised I would use it to help bridge a gap. I need one more year; then we will begin to self-feed ourselves."

He's not opposed to trading players, either. "We're going to be great historians," emphasized Steinbrenner. "We are not going to make the same mistakes the Yankees did in the past. They stayed with the great ones too long; and as inhuman as it may sound, you got to make sure you trade people at the peak time. And that's not easy to do. But one thing is certain, we're not going to get caught short."

He most certainly didn't by acquiring both veteran pitchers, the 35-year-old John and the 38-year-old Tiant. Psychologically, he upset the Boston Red Sox by signing Tiant. That's 13 victories the Sox will have to make up.

"So much of what goes on between the Yankees and the Red Sox is psychological," confided Boston catcher Carlton Fisk. "I never had the faintest worry that Tiant would not be with the Red Sox. I didn't think they could afford to let him go, especially to New York, to let a pitcher with talent and charisma slide through your fingers. It has nothing but a negative psychological impact on the Red Sox and a positive psychological impact on the Yankees."

It's a never-ending war. Somehow it seems that General Patton has cast his shadow over Yankee Stadium. George Steinbrenner would like that . . .

Thurman Munson and Pat Dobson with Billy Martin on his first day as manager, August 2, 1975.

2

Martin-Lemon

All he ever wanted was to be a Yankee. The passion consumed him. Down deep it overwhelmed him. His whole love for baseball was in the Yankees. Nothing else mattered. He wanted to be a Yankee badly, perhaps more than anyone else. He was a fighter. He had to be. All his life he had had to fight for survival. He learned how on the streets of Berkeley, California, where he grew up, raised by his mother and grandmother after his father had died. That's where his spirit came from. He had to learn to survive, to be somebody. And survive he did. He did so by scratching and clawing his way. Finally, on the day in 1950 when he became a Yankee for the first time, Billy Martin realized his life-long dream.

He joined the Yankees as an infielder. His credentials weren't exactly outstanding. He had played for Oakland in the Pacific Coast League for two years when he was 19 years old. He played hard, and he played to win.

The manager, Casey Stengel, liked the way he scrapped and hustled. He never forgot the brash youngster. Two years later, when he had a chance to get him, Stengel purchased Martin from Kansas City.

Stengel had a special liking for Martin. Perhaps he saw in the youngster the son he never had. In the seven years he played with the Yankees, Martin became known as "Casey's boy." He played both second base and shortstop, always with fierce determination. In his seven years as a Yankee, Martin batted .262 and hit only 30 home runs. Yet, Stengel wasn't afraid to bat Martin third when he returned to the club in 1955 following a two-year hitch in the Army. Martin responded by hitting .300

Still, it was for his fiery play in the World Series that Martin is best remembered. Martin saved the 1952 Series against the Brooklyn Dodgers for the Yanks. His defensive gem came in the seventh inning of the seventh game. With the bases loaded, Jackie Robinson hit a high pop fly near the pitcher's mound. It was the first baseman's play. Yet, Joe Collins never broke for the ball. At the last minute, Martin raced over and made an off-balance catch at his shoe tops to preserve the Yank's 4–2 victory.

But he also beat the Dodgers with his bat during the following year. Although he hit only .257 for the entire 1953 season, Martin was the batting star in the 1953 World Series. He set a record by collecting 12 hits in the six games, and he knocked in more runs—eight—than anybody on either team. He won the Babe Ruth Award as the most valuable player, finishing the series with a .500 average. He generated enough power to hit two home runs, two triples, and a double among his eight hits.

Although a great many players never seem to produce as expected during World Series play, Martin seemed to thrive on it. He loved the pressure and the challenge, and he responded. He had that something extra that winners seem to possess. In 28 World Series games, he hit .333 and belted five home runs. In the 133 plays he handled as a fielder, he was charged with only one error. Ironically, the year before he joined the Yankees, Martin led the Pacific Coast League in errors.

Martin's love affair with the Yankees cooled in 1957. At least the Yanks weren't enamored with Martin anymore. It wasn't a result of his play. Rather, it was an off-field incident that made the Yankee hierachy frown. In 1957 the Copacabana was a thriving nightclub, one of the "in" spots in New York. On the night of May 17, Martin was having a birthday celebration. Joining him were Mickey Mantle, Hank Bauer, Yogi Berra, Johnny Kucks, and their wives.

The night began in merriment. It wasn't until Martin and Bauer went to the restroom that the night exploded. Some intoxicated patron was bad-mouthing the Yankees. It didn't last very long. Martin and Bauer swooped down on him with a vengeance, and the fight made headlines the next day in the newspapers. The front office reacted. They felt it was conduct unbecoming a Yan-

Billy Martin during his playing days.

kee. Someone had to be made the scapegoat. It was Martin. Within a week he was traded to Kansas City despite Stengel's feelings.

Martin felt hurt. It was as if a part of him was dead. The next five years he bounced around from team to team—five, to be exact. After Kansas City came Detroit, Cleveland, Cincinnati, Milwaukee, and finally, Minnesota. They were a far cry from New York, away from his close buddies Mantle and Phil Rizzuto. Once more Martin had to survive. And again he managed.

In 1969 he was named manager of the Minnesota Twins and promptly led them to the Western Division championship. Martin was back, all right. But he didn't stay in Minnesota for long, only one year. He feuded with the front office and moved to Detroit. In 1972 he led the Tigers to the Eastern Division crown but was fired after the 1973 season began. A year later he sparked the Texas Rangers to a second place finish.

Catfish Hunter and Billy Martin, 1975

Turning around the Rangers as he did earned him the Associated Press Manager of the Year award.

But once more Martin had his disagreements with management. After the 1975 season got underway, Martin was replaced as manager of the Rangers by Frank Lucchesi. One thing was certain: Martin had all the fire and intensity he had possessed as a player. He proved he was a winner as manager as well. It was just that his relationship with the front office needed mellowing or perhaps understanding. Yet, in the dugout Martin showed that he could win.

Yankee owner George Steinbrenner noticed it, too. Like Martin, he strives to win, relentlessly championing for it. During that summer of 1975 the Yankees weren't winning enough. The year before, under Bill Virdon's first season, they had finished second. But it was now July; and it was apparent to Steinbrenner that the Yankees wouldn't win this year, either.

Like Martin, Virdon had played for the Yankees. Although he won the Eastern Division title when he managed the Pittsburgh Pirates in 1973, Virdon was not Steinbrenner's first choice to manage the Yankees for the 1974 season. Steinbrenner tried desperately to get Dick Williams who had fallen into disfavor with owner Charlie Finley at Oakland. When he couldn't, he agreed to hiring Virdon.

But the thought of getting Martin excited Steinbrenner. The Yankees weren't winning consistently, and attendance wasn't all that great. Why not get Martin, who had been a popular player with the fans of New York? Another reason that Steinbrenner wanted to move quickly was the fear that some other team might get to Martin first.

"Go sign him up, and we'll include Virdon out," Steinbrenner ordered Gabe Paul, who was president of the Yankees at the time.

"Are you sure you want this?" asked Paul. "Billy is pretty strong stuff, you know. Cal

Griffith couldn't take him, and neither could John Fetzer or Brad Corbett. When he was playing, seven different clubs shook him off."

"Milksops," snapped Steinbrenner. "I can take him or leave him alone. Get him for me."

Paul did. On August 1, Martin became manager of the Yankees. He was home again. He put on the Yankee pinstripes for the first time in 20 years. They still fit. They still were a part of him. When the season ended two months later, Martin had brought the Yankees in third.

But Martin was used to winning. That's the way he played. And he didn't wait long to win. In his first full season as manager in 1976, he brought a pennant to Yankee Stadium. That's what Steinbrenner liked, results. Before the season was over, he had given Martin a new three-year contract through the 1979 season.

Yet it was near the end of the season that the first signs of unrest surfaced between the two. Like Steinbrenner, Martin is strong-willed. And also like the owner, Martin demands respect. The two are almost of the same temperament, the same drive, the same obsession with winning. So it really isn't unusual if they don't agree on certain things, no matter how insignificant they may appear to an outsider.

Like the time in August when the Yankees were driving toward their first pennant in 12 years. Dick Williams—the same Dick Williams whom Steinbrenner first sought as a manager—was sitting with Steinbrenner in the owner's private box at Yankee Stadium. It caused speculation among the writers, naturally, since Williams was still unemployed. And naturally, word got back to Martin, who wasn't exactly overjoyed.

"Dick Williams is a friend of mine," explained Steinbrenner. "He has been since just before I tried to hire him. I got a call from a mutural friend one day saying Dick was in town and that he'd like to talk to me. I said, 'Fine, tell him to come to the game tonight.'

"Dick came, and we talked about his fu-

Billy Martin and Mickey Mantle on Old Timers' Day, 1975.

Billy Martin, 1977

ture. We never talked about him coaching or managing the Yankees. But Dick Williams is an outstanding baseball man and an outstanding person. He'd be an asset to our organization if we could find a place for him.

"Look, Billy and I have a rapport that few people have in sports. I've known him for 18 years. I've seen him go to Minnesota, Detroit, and Texas and do a hell of a job and get fired. I don't think that will happen here because I know Billy. I know how to get along with him. We joke with each other. I tell him he's No. 1½; I'm No. 1. He knows he's got to go along with the system.

"I told him that I didn't have Dick Williams here to embarrass him. I'm trying to run a company. The hardest thing in life is winning, and I'm trying to build an organization that will win. In a winning organization, nobody is indispensable. That goes for the manager, and that goes for me, too."

Martin felt embarrassed by Williams' presence. Perhaps it was rather a feeling of insecurity. After all, he had been fired from three different jobs, and he knew how much Steinbrenner respected Williams. Maybe he was a bit uneasy about it all.

"I told George that I thought he was a bigger man than that," said Martin. "I told him, 'You tick me off.' His taste was poor. He said he was just trying to get him a job in the organization. Well, I think there could have been another way to handle it that wouldn't embarrass me, but he's the boss. I don't know what he was trying to prove, but even if he hired Dick Williams, I wouldn't let it bother me.

"I'm not going to worry that he's got somebody waiting in the wings because there's always somebody waiting in the wings, whether he's working for your club or not. I never run scared, and I wasn't going to start now.

"I wanted three years on my contract for several reasons. I didn't even care about the money, but three years meant security, and it was a matter of pride. Three other clubs fired me, and they went around bad-mouthing me. I didn't fire Billy Martin; they fired Billy Martin. So why should they bad-mouth me? It was a matter of pride that after what they said about me, somebody was willing to give me a three-year contract. And I'm determined to prove that it was no mistake."

Although Martin led the Yankees to a pennant during his first season, they were totally victimized by the Cincinnati Reds in the World Series. The Reds swept the Yanks in four straight games. Over the winter, Steinbrenner made some moves in the free agent market that strengthened his club. He secured slugger Reggie Jackson from Baltimore and pitching ace Don Gullet from Cincinnati. He wanted a world championship.

So did Martin. That spring Martin felt that 1977 would be the Yankees' year, that they would go all the way for the first time since 1962. The addition of Jackson and Gullet was a definite plus. There was one negative issue: Would two strong-willed personalities like Jackson and Martin get along in the dugout?

For a while, they did. They even found time to joke with one another. But slowly their feelings toward one another began to cool. Jackson got off to a slow start, and the Yankees weren't exactly overpowering the rest of the league. At the end of May, they were only five games above .500, hardly a championship pace.

Jackson was looked upon as Steinbrenner's boy. The two often had private talks together. He was the prize. The rest of the players never warmed to Jackson. Steinbrenner insisted to Martin that Jackson should bat fourth. Martin refused. Even though Steinbrenner was the owner, Martin felt he was in charge of the team. Martin began to look at Jackson with mistrust.

It was like a powder keg waiting to explode. All that was needed was a spark. That's how volatile the situation had become. The explosion finally occurred in June on national television while the Yankees were playing the Red Sox in Boston. Irate because he felt that Jackson had loafed in going after a ball that Jim Rice had hit, Martin yanked his controversial rightfielder out of the game.

Jackson was stunned by the move. As he came running off the field and into the dugout, he had words with Martin.

Martin erupted. He wanted to go after Jackson. He had to be restrained from attacking Jackson by a couple of his coaches, Yogi Berra and Elston Howard. It wasn't a pleasant scene. The television audience had a closeup view of a near-fight.

Steinbrenner didn't like what he saw, either. He moved quickly to quell any hostility that could spread throughout the entire team. He flew to Detroit the very next day and had late-night meetings with Jackson, Martin, and the team's captain, Thurman Munson. Tempers cooled, at least for that moment.

In August, Martin finally relented and positioned Jackson fourth in the batting order. The Yankees went on a tear. At the end of

The 1977 World Series Clubhouse.

July they were only 13 games above .500. By the end of August, however, they were 28 games above break even. They were in first place by four games and driving toward a second straight pennant.

Peace seemed to have settled on the Yankees. The Yanks won the pennant and then went on to defeat the Los Angeles Dodgers in six games in the World Series. It was a series that will be remembered as Jackson's. He blasted three home runs in the final game to earn a place in World Series history, right alongside the immortal Babe Ruth. Still, he set a World Series record for the most home runs, five in a six-game series.

When the Yankees reported to spring training before the 1978 season, they appeared even stronger. Martin acquired some additional bullpen strength when Steinbrenner picked up Rich Gossage in the free agent market. Gossage, who was with the Pittsburgh Pirates the year before, was considered one of the best relievers in the National League.

Still, the Yankees' problems continued to abound. With Gossage's presence, Sparky Lyle became unhappy. The rest of the players were still a bit uneasy with Jackson. The sensitive Jackson felt it. As slowly as the Yanks started in 1977, they got off to an even worse start this year.

Once again tempers were mounting. Some felt that Martin was losing control of the club. Losing did not improve his personality. He became testy and irritable. Once more the Yankee clubhouse was a powder keg, and once more all that was needed to set off an explosion was a spark.

It came in July, one month later than in the previous year. Almost prophetic was the fact

that once again Jackson lit the flame. This time there was no mistaking the fact that Jackson was wrong. He defied Martin's orders to swing away. On one pitch he disregarded the sign from third base coach Dick Howser. Then on the next pitch he disobeyed the coach's verbal orders.

Immediately after the game, Martin suspended Jackson. Martin's move had the complete support of management. Steinbrenner and club president Al Rosen publicly supported Martin's action. Jackson was suspended for five games without pay. Not only did Jackson incur Martin's wrath, but his teammates also were annoyed.

At the time, the Yankees fell 14 games behind the Red Sox. But during the time that Jackson was gone from the club, the Yanks won five straight and trimmed Boston's margin to 10½ games. Unfortunately, the strain that Martin was under overtook him.

Jackson returned to the club on Sunday. That night, as the team was leaving Chicago for Kansas City, Martin made some inflammatory remarks regarding Jackson. What was worse was that he included Steinbrenner. He called Jackson a born liar and Steinbrenner a convicted one. Martin, who was always tough and hard, had cracked.

He was finished and he knew it. The question was how to leave. The Yankees let him resign the next day in Kansas City. In a tearful resignation statement that he couldn't finish, Martin bid his farewell to the Yankees on July 24. His dream had shattered into little pieces. His whole world had crumbled. For the first time in his life, Billy Martin quit.

It was up to Bob Lemon to pick up the pieces. Just 28 hours after Martin's tearful exodus, Lemon was named manager of the beleaguered Yankees. Ironically, he had been Martin's pitching coach the year before. Even more ironic was that he had been fired as manager of the Chicago White Sox a month before. He had done an excellent job in Chicago in 1977. He led the White Sox to a third place finish which earned him manager of the year honors. But in 1978, the White Sox were losing, so the unpredictable Bill

Veeck, owner of the team, fired Lemon and replaced him with Larry Doby.

Lemon was a good friend of Rosen. That made it easier. Rosen sent out a distress call to Lemon at his California home, and Lemon agreed to manage the Yankees. Terms and salary were not discussed. But that's the way Lemon is. He is the extreme opposite of Martin in size and disposition. In a large sense he is a secure individual. He didn't worry about a contract at that particular moment.

The mild-tempered Lemon had excellent credentials. He was a member of the Hall of Fame, a fierce competitor in the years he pitched for the Cleveland Indians. He was low-keyed in his approach, whether pitching or managing, and nobody in baseball had a bad word to say about him. Although he appeared easygoing on the surface, he was

Bob Lemon

tough inside. He approached whatever task he faced simply and honestly, without any melodramatic emotions or overworked theories.

"I know Billy was a favorite, and he's going to be a tough act to follow," said Lemon when he took the job. "He's been successful. He's always been my friend. We played together, barnstormed together, and went to Japan together. I have a great deal of respect for him; and I know that the fans do, too. I imagine there will be negative reaction somewhere down the line.

"I've got 40 years of baseball, and being a manager is the closest thing to being on the field, to being in the ball game itself. We haven't talked contract yet. I don't know if I'm here on a daily, weekly, or monthly basis. But I didn't take this job on an interim basis. I could have stayed home and drawn pretty good money from the White Sox sitting on my butt. My wife is tough but probably not as tough as the New York fans. I just hope we can win some games so there can be no doubt who manages the team next year.

"I'm going to tell the players how I feel. I'll treat them like men as long as they let me. Ball players make their own rules. If they act like children, we can treat them like children. I'm just going to take it from there. They are all superstars here. I've never had this type of talent before. What we have to do depends on what the other teams do. I don't think Boston has won it yet. It could be interesting."

Taking over the Yankees was Lemon's third managerial job. In his first managerial position in 1970, he was placed in charge of the one-year-old Kansas City Royals, an expansion team. He led them to a second place finish in 1971. After the Royals dropped to fourth place in 1972, Lemon was fired. Royals owner Ewing Kauffman let Lemon go because he felt he was too old and wanted someone who was in closer touch with the younger generation.

Now, six years later, at the age of 58, Lemon was asked to manage a team of stars and superstars, many of whom were spoiled and highly sensitive. It wasn't exactly the Garden of Eden. As quiet and unassuming as he appears, Lemon nevertheless knew that he was being asked to bring calm and peace to a team of complete unrest.

"I'm not going to comment on any past difficulties involving Martin and the players," explained Lemon. "I wasn't involved. I'm coming in here with an open mind. Twenty minutes after I get here I might have something to say. Right now I haven't experienced problems. It's just that everything is just more magnified in New York. I'm not going to pass judgment on ball players until I have had a chance to deal with them.

"I can take constructive criticism. When it comes down to it, the coaches help me, but I make the decisions. Anybody can make suggestions to you, but the last say should be the manager's. I don't think there should be any secrets between the managers and the coaches and the front office. I think there's a way to work it out."

Along with Rosen, Cedric Tallis, the Yankees' general manager, was an admirer of Lemon. Tallis had been at Kansas City when Lemon managed there.

"The man who won 20 games seven times just acts like he was anybody," remarked Tallis. "That's the remarkable thing about Lemon. He has never really sold himself. He's the placid type, and he never has been one to tell you how good he was. In all the years I've known Bob Lemon, I never can recall him telling anything about his career, particularly anything he did well. He never bragged on himself. He might tell you some embarrassing situation where he got racked up.

"He's the type of manager that if he has something to tell you, he'll tell you, but on the side. He won't embarrass you. He will make the ultimate use of his coaches. I think that if you can't play for Lemon, then you can't play for anybody."

It was Tallis who got Lemon his first major league job at Kansas City. It was Tallis who also objected when Kauffman fired Lemon after just 2½ years on the job. During those

years, Yankee outfielder Lou Piniella played under Lemon. He knew what to expect from Lemon.

"He's a tough dude," snapped Piniella. "He'll fool you with that placid smile and soft disposition. Tough dude. He just looks you in the eye and wants to know what's going on. Why aren't you hustling?

"But he's easy to play for, easy to get along with. He just expects you to hustle and will never criticize you if you do. Yet, as quiet as he is, he's surprisingly tough. Don't cross him or he'll have you in his office in two minutes, chewing you out and taking some of your money. As you get older and look back you realize that it was for your own good."

Rosen goes back even farther with Lemon. He was Lemon's teammate when they both played for Cleveland some 30 years ago. Yet, Rosen's earliest recollection of Lemon goes back to 1941 at spring training in Sumter, South Carolina, when Rosen was trying to make the Indians' Wilkes-Barre, Pennsylvania, club.

"Lemon was on the table in the clubhouse moaning and groaning in pain," began Rosen. "He had been pitching batting practice and got hit in the groin without a cup. I got to know him better when I joined the Indians. He was a student but never overbearing with advice.

"For instance, he told me one time in his way, 'You know, I'd like to pitch against you sometime.' It was his way of telling me that I was too much of a first-ball hitter. 'You would never get a strike on the first pitch from me,' he would say, instead of saying the obvious, 'You swing at the first pitch all the time!' When I asked him why that was important, he said that pitchers all over the league know that I jump all over the first pitch, which helped me. That was when I first came up.

"He was always a guy who could bring a degree of levity to a situation. He could say something that would get everybody laughing. If I said the same things, somebody would have been offended. You've seen people like that. He was truly a leader. If he was in the john on the train, he gathered a crowd. There was some doubt at the time that he could be a manager because it was thought that he might have too much empathy with the players. But when he got his shot, he was a good one even though the clubs he's had weren't outstanding. He knew pitching, which was a real plus. I've always felt that Lemon is a completely unflappable man."

He would have to be, considering the situation he was walking into. There were a lot of raised eyebrows when Lemon was announced as the new manager. After all, less than a month before he was fired at Chicago. He was well aware of the atmosphere around the Yankees.

"It's the best ballclub I've been able to manage," exclaimed Lemon. "I don't care if they call me a caretaker or housesitter or whatever. I grew up with a name like Lemon, and I've taken a lot of abuse. I love to manage. But you can't compare my love and Billy's. He grew up here. This is where he belongs.

"I don't get too high, and I don't get too low. You let youself get carried away and then when things blow up you wind up with your head down. I never took a game home with me. I always left it in some bar. Why did I come back to manage the Yankees? Because Al Rosen asked me, and Al is a friend. I try to let my personality guide me and hope some of it rubs off on the players.

"You're always aware of things the manager is doing over the years. It has to go through your mind. Then, years later, when you become a manager, you realize you've borrowed some things from all the ones you've played for, in the minors as well as in the majors. You get some dos and don'ts from everybody.

"You need to have a rapport with your players. In our days, we didn't turn to the front office, but the game is different now. It's a game of individuals, and they have to display themselves in different ways."

Lemon was indeed a man who moved with the times. Today's modern players didn't pass him by. On a road trip taken shortly after he assumed command, one of the Yankee regulars came to Lemon's hotel room. He griped that he was tired, that he was seeing too much action and wanted some time off. Lemon looked up at him from behind his glasses.

"Look, Meat," began Lemon, using his favorite name for players he has a liking for. "I don't know what's in your contract. I don't know how much money you are making, and I don't give a damn. I'm trying to win this thing, and it doesn't take a damn genius to see that the guys who won it last year are the players I want in the lineup. You got any gripes, you take them upstairs. As long as I am manager and I think you belong in the starting lineup, you'll damn well be in the starting lineup."

Lemon doesn't beat around the bush. He admits he is lazy in that respect and doesn't like to mince words. It takes too long. He likes to make his point plainly and quickly.

Like one time in Cleveland. Lou Piniella and Thurman Munson were frustrated at making outs and threw their helmets toward the Yankee dugout in anger. Lemon had to duck to avoid being hit. After the game he closed the clubhouse to outsiders and spoke to the entire team.

"There will be no breaking bats and throwing helmets like that anymore," lectured Lemon. "That includes everybody and anybody, and I do mean *anybody!*"

He got the message across. And if any individual players tested him, he made certain that they knew he meant business, especially if they broke any rules. That he wouldn't condone. Mickey Rivers and Roy White found that out twice! When they arrived an hour late for a game in Seattle, he fined them. When they did the same thing in Cleveland, he fined both of them a second time. And when a reporter found out about the fines and wanted to know how much they were penalized, Lemon wouldn't say.

"That's none of your damn business," he barked. "That's a team matter. It's between me and the players."

It was his way of not embarrassing his players. That's one thing he never does. By the same token, he doesn't like to get embarrassed, either. Because of his easygoing nature, some players may look upon him as an easy target. But he's not easily fooled, as Reggie Jackson discovered one night in Baltimore.

Lemon penciled Jackson's name in the eighth spot in the batting order. Jackson told Lemon that he didn't feel good and couldn't play. Lemon just shrugged and didn't say anything more.

"If a player tells me he's sick, he's sick," exclaimed Lemon.

The next day Jackson batted seventh. Lemon made his point quietly and firmly. That's his style.

"All I want is 1979," remarked Lemon. "That will make 42 years I've been in uniform, and that's enough. On the field is still okay; but all the traveling and the media, I've had enough of that."

The door was left open for Billy Martin's return. After all, he is a traveling man. He hasn't had enough . . .

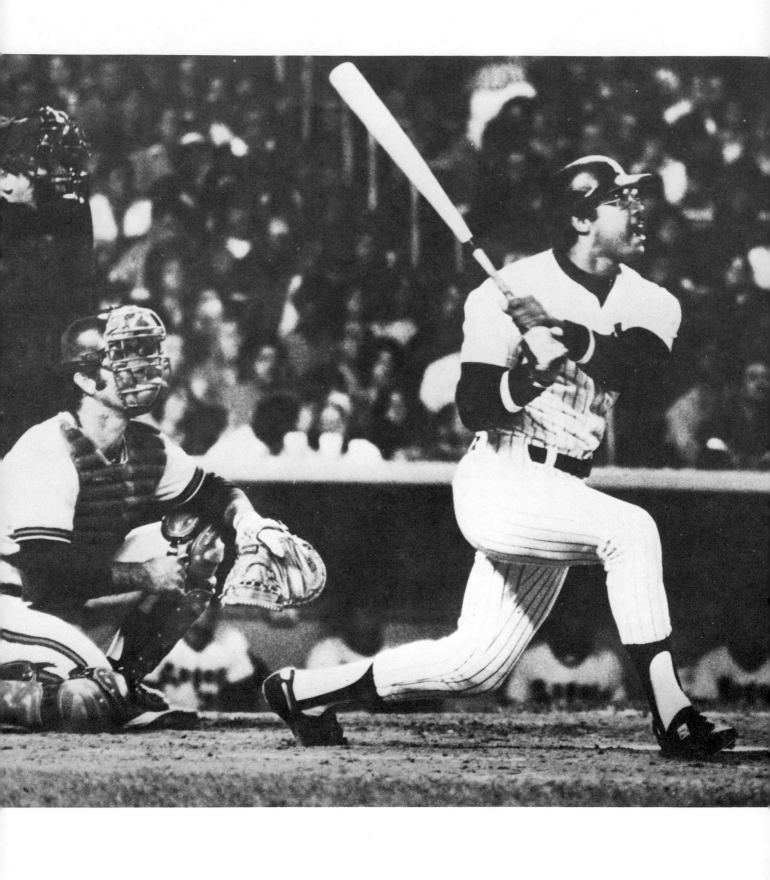

3

Reggie Jackson

It was a bad beginning. Somehow he never belonged. He felt alienated. Down deep, he really didn't feel part of the team. It's a lonely feeling. It could nurture hostility and unrest. The Yankee pinstripes were new to him. Before that he wore the uniforms of the Oakland Athletics and the Baltimore Orioles. He harvested his fame in Oakland where he played in two World Series. Baltimore was only a stopover less than one season long. He never really wanted to go to Baltimore. What he desired was New York; and when Reggie Jackson joined the New York Yankees for the first time in the spring of 1977, his reputation preceded him.

Everyone in baseball knew what he could do with a bat. That was his weapon. He could swing it with awesome power—the long ball, the big hit. His command of the bat compensated for his shortcomings in the outfield. Not that he is a horrible fielder, but he's no All-Star when it comes to the glove. But that

wasn't where it was at for Jackson anyway. He was the menacing slugger with the classic swing. Certainly, no other hitter in the game had more flair for dramatics than Jackson.

But he also had a capacity for creating excitement off the field. He is a flashy dresser who likes expensive commodities like cars, clothes, and homes. He always moved around in the best circles, restaurants, society, and such. He is handsome, an eligible bachelor. Being articulate and intelligent makes him that much more attractive. He is easily recognizable in a crowd because he has that rare trait that all great athletes possess, charisma. And what better place than New York for someone like Jackson? Oakland and Baltimore were just bus stops along the way. He has an awareness of where it's at.

"I'm not merely a baseball player," remarked Jackson. "I am a black man who has done what he wants, gotten what he wanted, and will continue to get it. Now what I want

to do is to develop my intellect. You see, on the field I am a surgeon. I put on my glove and hat and shoes. And I go out on the field and I cut up the other team.

"I am a surgeon. No one can quite do it the way I do. But off the field, I try to forget all about it. You know, you can get very narrow being a superstar. I mean being a superstar can make life very difficult. Difficult to grow. So I visit with my friends, listen to some fine music, drink some good wine, perhaps take a ride in the country in a fine car, or just walk along the beach. Nature is extremely important to me, which may be just about the only trouble I'll have in New York. I'll miss the trees."

But the trouble he experienced went far beyond the trees. It was a very uneasy spring for Jackson. Maybe he came on too strong. Perhaps he put himself above everyone else. Certainly his newly signed contract did. Jackson was the prize in the free agent market that winter. The Yankees signed him to a $2.9 million contract making him the most highly paid Yankee other than Catfish Hunter. While his signing made headlines all over the country, other Yankee players like Thurman Munson, Sparky Lyle, and Graig Nettles sulked a bit. They had been seeking more money; and in one swoop, Jackson seemed to have taken it all.

It wasn't that Jackson was joining a bunch of losers. Far from it. In 1976 the Yankees swept to the American League pennant, only to lose to the Cincinnati Reds in the World Series in four straight games. Nothing rankled owner George Steinbrenner more than the ignominious defeat in the fall classic. So Steinbrenner determinedly turned to the free agent market and signed Jackson and pitcher Don Gullett, who had beaten the Yankees in the Series, among others.

The Yankee players never warmed to Jackson during his first spring. And Jackson never tried hard to win his new teammates over. He was the new kid on the block, brash and gaudy. The other Yankees kept their distance. They appeared to be defensive even though they weren't withdrawn. It's just that they said little and never openly embraced

their new teammate. Perhaps Jackson came on too strong. Perhaps his personality was too abrasive. At any rate, Jackson was not the savior he was represented to be. The Yankees had won without him, and they were convinced that they could do it again.

"I don't think we need him," exclaimed Lyle, who was in a heated dispute with management regarding money. "Not to take anything away from his talents, but what we really needed was a good right-handed hitter, a right-handed superstar."

Such remarks cut Jackson. He is very sensitive. He needs to feel wanted. Jackson felt the tension in the atmosphere. Every so often he tried to make with the small talk, just to make contact. But it was nothing more than superficial conversation. There was no heavy talk, no sitting down privately and seeing where it was at with the others. That's not Jackson's style.

"You know, this team, it all flows from me," emphasized Jackson. "I've got to keep it all going. I'm the straw that stirs the drink. It all comes back to me. Maybe I should say me and Munson, but really he doesn't enter into it. He's being so damned insecure about the whole thing. I've overheard him talking about me. I'll hear him telling some other writer that he wants it to be known that he's the captain of the team, that he knows what's best. Stuff like that. And when anybody knocks me, he'll laugh real loud so I can hear it."

The underlying currents were already stirring. Yet, nobody took the time to smooth the waters. No one wanted to take a step toward clearing the air, so to speak. Munson, too, had pride. He was the guts of the Yankees. He was an all-star, the good catcher with the good bat. In 1976 he was voted the league's most valuable player. That's saying it all.

It was understandable why he looked upon Jackson as a stranger, an intruder. Jackson isn't the most subtle person in the world. He can appear unapproachable at times. And as strong-willed as Jackson was, so, too, was Munson. The two never met halfway just to talk and respect each other's presence.

Reggie Jackson with Jim Wynn,
1977.

(Below) Jackson hugs his father, Martinez, after hitting three home runs in the 1977 World Series.

"He's not ready for it," disclosed Jackson. "He doesn't even know he feels like he does. He isn't aware of it yet. He'd say, 'What? I'm not jealous. There aren't any problems.' He'd try to cover up, but he ought to know he can't cover up anything from me. I can read these guys. No, I'll wait and eventually he'll be whipped. There will come that moment when he really knows I've won. And he'll want to hear everything is all right; and then I'll go to him, and we'll get it right."

Heavy. It most certainly didn't alleviate the tension. If anything, it caused Munson and many others to withdraw. Yet, it could have been avoided. But nobody seemed capable of communicating with one another. That's where it was all at. But the sniping persisted, and it only got worse. Jackson felt the need to establish himself. It just didn't work the way he presented it. He wasn't going to come in and leave his new teammates awe-stricken. No chance of that at all.

"Well, that is part of my problem," confided Jackson. "I do everything as honestly as I can. I give all I have to give. But I don't let people get in my way. You see, that is the way I am. I'm a leader, and I can't lie down. But leader isn't the right word. It's a matter of presence.

"Let me put it this way: No team that I am on will ever be humiliated the way the Yankees were by the Reds in the World Series! That's why Munson can't intimidate me. Nobody can. You can't psyche me. You take me one-on-one in the pit, and I'll whip you. It's an attitude, really. It's the way the manager looks at you when you come into the room. It's the way the coaches and the batboy look at you. The way your name trickles through the crowd when you wait in the batter's box. It's all that.

"The way the Yankees were humiliated by the Reds. You think that doesn't bother Billy Martin? He's no fool. He's smart. Very smart. And he's a winner. Munson's tough, too. He is a winner, but there is just nobody who can do for a club what I can do. There is nobody who can put fans in the stands the way I can. That's just the way it is. Munson thinks he can be the straw that stirs the drink, but he can only stir it bad."

Strong. But that's Jackson's way. It's that it wouldn't work with this club. It was a championship team. In just two years, Martin led them to a pennant. Yankee pride and a sense of accomplishment returned. When they won a pennant in 1976, it was the first time it had happened in 12 years. That's a long time. In the rich Yankee history that is synonymous with championships, it was too long.

"Martin has presence, too," observed Jackson. "He's no dummy. I can feel him letting me do what I want, then roping me in whenever he needs to. But I'll make it easy for him. He won't have to be 'bad' Billy Martin fighting people anymore. He can move up a notch because I'll open the road, and I'll let the others come thundering down the path.

"The rest of the guys should know that I don't feel that far above them. I mean, nobody can turn people on like I can or do for a club the things that I can do, but we are all still athletes; we're all still ball players. We should be able to get along. We've got a strong common ground, common wants.

"I'm not going to let the small stuff get in the way. But if that's not enough, then I'll be gone. A friend of mine has already told me: 'You or Munson will be gone in two years.' I really don't want that to be the case because after all is said and done, Munson is a winner, he's a fighter, a hell of a ball player. But don't you see, there is no way that I can play second fiddle to anybody. That's just not in the cards. There ain't no way."

Dynamite. It appeared as if the Yankee unrest of that spring would explode even before the season began. Strangely, nobody seemed sufficiently aware of the situation to soothe it. The feeling among players probably is that once a game begins, everybody forgets about any problems. But what was happening at this time went far beyond the playing fields. No one seemed to understand that.

The only player who had had any previous contact with Jackson was Hunter. They had played together on the world championship

Manager Billy Martin is restrained by Elston Howard and Yogi Berra during a shouting match with Reggie Jackson in Boston in 1977. (Wide World Photos)

Oakland teams. It was Hunter who first made it big in the free agent market, who first harvested the big dollars. He had a respect for Jackson's talents.

"Reggie is a team leader," explained Hunter. "I mean he can get hot with his bat and carry a team for three weeks. He's ready to go all the time. The thing you have to understand about Reggie is that he wants everyone to love him."

It never happened. The bitter seeds of spring never sweetened once the season began. Jackson was uncomfortable. He still wasn't accepted by his teammates. The atmosphere in the clubhouse wasn't all that good. Jackson himself got off to a slow start. The Yankee fans began to boo him. He heard the boos, and it hurt him. There he was, a new player in town, and now the fans as well as his teammates made him feel unwelcome.

Near the end of June, the tension on the team began to surface. The Yankees were not playing well as a team and were in second place. Reports were abounding that there were problems on the team, basically among the players themselves. Like Jackson, Martin is strong-minded. He tried to squash the stories, almost to the point of being nonchalant.

"Without me they could win, but there would be a lot of problems," snapped Martin. "I'm the right guy for the right team. I won last year, remember?"

But this was another year, one that brought Jackson to the team for the first time. There was coolness among the players, and there were personal conflicts, some extending into private arguments. It finally erupted into open hostility before a national television audience in Boston.

Red Sox slugger Jim Rice drove a ball safely into rightfield. Jackson ran after the ball, picked it up, and threw it back to the infield. However, Rice had safely made it to second base. Angered, Martin sent in Paul Blair to replace Jackson.

A shocked Jackson returned to the dugout. While he was still descending the steps, Martin angrily lashed out at him. Every television viewer saw what was taking place. Martin explained later that he felt that Jackson had not hustled after the ball, allowing Rice to take an extra base. Jackson felt hurt and humiliated. Steinbrenner felt a tempest brewing in a tea pot.

When the Yankees arrived in Detroit the following night, Steinbrenner was there. Many felt that Martin would be fired. Yet, it was Jackson who appealed on Martin's behalf. Others felt that the only reason that Steinbrenner didn't fire Martin then was that there weren't any satisfactory replacements available.

"You never did like me," charged Jackson to Martin. "Nothing I could do would ever please you."

The season had been a nightmare for Jackson. Where earlier he had talked freely with reporters, he now avoided them. He had an explanation, too.

"I don't want any interviews," he demanded. "I'm entitled to not getting ripped all the time."

But pitcher Ken Holtzman had an explanation of Jackson's change. He, too, had been a

teammate of Jackson on the same team at Oakland, the colorful, bickering Athletics who somehow managed to win championships. He felt the media pressure was too much for Jackson.

"Most successful major leaguers learn to block out that aspect," offered Holtzman. "One of the most difficult adjustments is the switch from relative obscurity to total recognition. If this team were playing in Oakland with one full-time reporter, you wouldn't hear nearly what you do here. The interaction would be the same among the players, but it wouldn't be magnified as it has. That tends to strain the emotions of certain players."

When a team isn't winning, the players become grumpy. Tempers are short. Even good-natured kidding, such as what takes place on bus rides to and from the airport, can erupt into arguments. Like one such incident between Jackson and centerfielder Mickey Rivers. A truck passed the Yankee bus, and Jackson saw it.

"There goes Rivers in five years, driving a truck," remarked Jackson.

"Yeah, but I'll be happy driving a truck," answered Rivers.

"Listen to me arguing with a guy who can't read or write," snapped Jackson.

"You better stop reading and writing and start hitting," charged Rivers.

The players were losing their sense of humor. When that happens, it can only lead to more trouble. Everybody seemed to recognize it, but no one did anything constructive to clear the air. The one missing link was someone to pull the players together. Now, instead of sitting in the middle of the bus, Jackson preferred to sit up front where it was quiet.

"That's what ball players do, they say things," explained outfielder Lou Piniella. "Reggie takes it too personally."

"The first thing for the players who have salary disputes to jump on was Reggie," remarked Munson. "Reggie took it personally when it really may have been directed at the owner."

"He's making all that money and ain't helped us win," snapped Rivers. "The guys who helped us win, they ain't signed."

Somehow the Yankees pulled together for the remainder of the season. It wasn't due to any single factor except pride. Jackson started to hit with more consistency. By the end of August the Yankees had moved into first place and pulled four games in front. When the season ended, they had won 100 games, winning the Eastern Division by 2½ games over Boston and Baltimore.

Jackson finished the year with a .286 batting average. He provided the long ball with 32 home runs and 110 runs batted in. The credentials are supple when considering that Jackson did indeed get off to a slow start. He, more than anyone, displayed fierce pride.

Yet, in the five-game championship play-off series against the Kansas City Royals, Jackson fell into a slump. He batted only .125, getting only two hits in 16 times at bat. Neither of the two hits was a home run.

However, there was still the World Series against the Los Angeles Dodgers. It turned out to be Jackson's finest hour as a Yankee. In fact, it was the greatest one-game hitting performance by any player in World Series history.

Jackson had recovered his batting eye. After five games, the Yankees led, 3–2. In those five games, Jackson batted .353. He had six hits in 17 times at bat, two of the safeties being home runs. But in the sixth game, he was something else. He gave perhaps the most memorable performance in history. The 56,407 fans in Yankee Stadium came to see Jackson hit, and hit he did.

When he got up in the second inning for the first time, the Yankees were behind, 2–0. Jackson walked, and then Chris Chambliss immediately tied the game with a home run. It wasn't until his next time at bat in the fourth inning that Jackson started the fans cheering.

This time the Yanks were trailing 3–2. Munson opened the inning with a single. Jackson quickly sent the Yanks in front when he drilled the first pitch from starter Burt Hooton into the lower rightfield stands. The Yankees added another run to increase their lead to 5–3.

It didn't remain that way long. In the fifth inning Rivers led off with a single. Willie Randolph, attempting to sacrifice, forced him at second base. One out later Randolph was still on first base as Jackson came up. Once more Jackson didn't wait long. He swung on the first pitch from reliever Elias Sosa and deposited it once again into the rightfield seats and opened the Yanks' lead to 7–3.

Jackson had one more at bat. He was the first batter up in the eighth inning, facing knuckleballer Charlie Hough for the first time. He treated Hough the same way he did Hooton and Sosa. Jackson swung on the first pitch and sent a monumental home run soaring into the centerfield bleachers. The ball was hit with such authority that it traveled about 500 feet.

As Jackson ran around the bases he was smiling at the standing ovation he received from the delirious fans. They had booed him earlier in the season, but they were applauding his heroics now, screaming, "Reggie, Reggie, Reggie!" It was the third time in Series history that anyone ever hit three homers in one game. Actually, Jackson was the second player to do it, the legendary Babe Ruth accomplishing the feat twice.

It was a great relief for Jackson. With only three swings of the bat he had vindicated an entire season. In the noisy celebration that was the Yankees' clubhouse, Jackson, as always, was the center of attention.

"Those three homers, they made me feel, at least for one night, like a real superstar," exclaimed Jackson. "I knew I'd be able to breathe again. Those home runs delivered a simple message: Let me up now; I'm no longer going to be held down.

"I'm not Joe DiMaggio and I'm not Babe Ruth. Those guys were great, great baseball players. DiMaggio is a living legend. The Yankee Clipper. I know he has been pulling for me. He came over to the dugout before the game when he threw out the first ball.

"I was humiliated by sportswriters, embarrassed by my manager, treated badly by my teammates. I was called egotistical and selfish. I had to prove myself to everybody day after day, game after game. But I guess I finally did it."

Yet despite the melodrama, there was still an undercurrent in the Series. Despite the fact that the Yankees won in six games, there was still a trace of animosity. One game's heroics aren't enough to remove the stigma of ill will.

Like after the second game of the Series. After the Yankees won the opening game, Martin started Hunter, who had had arm trouble most of the year. He lasted less than three innings, being raked for five runs in the Dodgers' 6–1 triumph. Surrounded by reporters, Jackson opened a volatile subject.

"How could he pitch a sore-armed pitcher in a game like this?" asked Jackson.

Martin wasn't aware of the criticism until it was revealed to him later. Naturally, he bristled. Jackson had hit a raw nerve.

"He has enough trouble in rightfield," snapped Martin. "A true Yankee doesn't criticize another Yankee player or the manager. We're all supposed to be working together to win. The way to do it is not with the mouth but with a bat and glove.

"But why should I pay attention to him anyway? His teammates don't. Did I criticize him the other day when he didn't run after a fly ball? Mickey Rivers had to come over from centerfield to get it. If I'm gonna back him, why doesn't he back me? It's a two-way street. He's a man of moods. Too bad it has to be this way. In Oakland, I know they had a tendency to criticize the manager; but here the manager runs the club, and he should have learned that by now."

But in the winter months Jackson only learned about what he would do the next season. He was still upset by what took place in 1977. And he promised himself that it would not happen again. He knew he could not endure another season like 1977. The sweet ending of the World Series was disturbed only by the bitter memories of the entire season.

"I'm not gonna be messed with this year," warned Jackson. "I'm not taking anything from my teammates. Things are gonna be different in 1978. If anyone gives me trouble, I'll be patient. I'll wait until I can get them alone. I know when they'll be alone. Maybe after the game on the way to the bus, or in an elevator at the hotel. Wherever it is, I'm gonna stop them and say, 'You aren't going to crap on me this year. I'm this close to blowing up. Don't mess with me or I'll tear you apart.'

"It's hard to understand unless you've lived through what I did last year. I almost cracked up. I couldn't understand it. It was horrible, rotten. Anything I got, they'd say, 'The nigger doesn't deserve it. He never hit .300.' They see me working hard on my defense; and they say, 'The nigger's a show-boat.' They see me sign autographs for two or three hours, and they say, 'The nigger just wants his name in the papers.'

"Do they ever say, 'The nigger can play!'? That he wins? That he performs under pressure? Do they look at what I withstood and say, 'That nigger has fiber?' Just once I'd like to hear that. I'd like to hear someone say, 'Thanks, thanks for playing your butt off.' No, it's always, 'What's wrong with Reggie? He's a phony, not real, a glory hound, a manipulator.' Why doesn't anybody say, 'The man can do it; he goes out and does it.'?

"Honest to God in Heaven, I didn't think it would be like that. You think I would have gone to the Yankees if I knew? Think a person wants to be disliked? I thought guys would say, 'Here's a guy who played in the Series. He can help us. Let's go along with his program because he's been there.'

"I missed it by 180 degrees. But it would have been easy to lay down and die, and I didn't. Those homers, they told there was a God in Heaven. They told me more about my character than my talent. You can't believe the pressure. You can't believe what it's like putting on that 44 and hearing them say, 'Go.'"

Jackson looked back, and he looked ahead to the 1978 season. He felt he was more aware of what was around him. Yet, the camaraderie with his teammates wasn't there. He felt more comfortable, more at ease with players from the other teams. With them he would make small talk and even joke around the batting cage. Down deep he only hoped that it would be that way with his teammates. Despite the dawn of a new season, things remained the same.

"In the locker room I don't feel like I'm one of the guys," admitted Jackson. "It's hard for me to say this. I'd like to fit in, but I don't know if I'll ever really be allowed to fit. I need to be appreciated, even praised. I like to hear, 'Nice going. Great going. You're a helluva ball player.' But I walk in feeling disliked. Maybe I'm overdoing it. Like I never get on anybody in the clubhouse unless it's a situation where it's obvious that it's okay for me to say something. I stay in the background. I never talk to too many people.

"I never small talk with anyone. I don't feel that anyone wants to talk to me. So I kind of shut up. I'm always the one who has to initiate the conversation. Sometimes I hear my voice in the locker room, and I want to take it back. I don't want anyone to look at me or feel uncomfortable around me."

It was strange. Jackson, a bona fide superstar, was still searching for answers. He had it all, the good life that so many others dream about. He owned three Rolls Royces, and his World Series heroics earned him more business deals. One that he was particularly fond of was having a candy bar, "Reggie," named after him. Just like Babe Ruth. He couldn't ask for anything more. All he wanted was to feel that he belonged with his teammates. That was the vacuum he faced.

All he could hope was that his teammates would come to understand him, to know him like Hunter and Holtzman do from their days at Oakland. Even in those halcyon years there was fun in the clubhouse. And what made it better was that they won.

"In 1977, the players didn't understand how Reggie could have the kind of first half he had and still keep talking," explained Hunter. "It was the same at Oakland. You've got to disregard two-thirds of what you read in print that Reggie said. If you don't, he can really play with your head. Only about one-third matters, anyway. The rest is just Reggie talking. What I think is that he tries too hard to be liked, and somewhere along the line it comes out wrong."

Perhaps Jackson is misunderstood. Maybe others don't want to take the time to understand him. He is basically a complex individual. But he is also a person with sensitivity, one with deep feelings and convictions. Jackson believes that people don't understand him.

"I wish someone would sit down with me quietly and try to find out what's inside of me, what my motivations are, what makes Reggie Jackson tick," insists Jackson. "Every-

body thinks I'm mercenary, self-centered, on an ego trip. Everybody is so wrong. Ego trip, hell. I don't give a damn about ego. That's the trouble. Nobody understands what drives me. Nobody knows my basic philosophy.

"What drives me is my obligation to myself and to God. God gave me talent. It's my duty to give something back. I don't draw a lot of personal pleasure from doing what I did in the Series. I was paid a lot of money. I was expected to do it. Two home runs, they were what I owed. The third one was a lucky bonus.

"It hurts me when people say I am inter-ested only in money and myself. People relate everything to the dollar. They never look inside a man to see the sensitivity, emotion, feeling, and concern that rest there. That's sad. When they write the obituary on Reggie Jackson, I don't want them to say he was a great home run hitter. I would like them to say he was a helluva person. He lived up to what God expected him to do.

"I feel a great responsibility to kids, to my teammates, management, fans, friends, and family. Me? I come last. Who understands that?"

Possibly no one . . .

Here's what Reggie Jackson did in the 1977 World Series:

- Hit three home runs in consecutive at-bats, drove in five runs and scored four in the final game.
- Homered his last time up in game No. 5 and walked on four pitches his first time up in game No. 6. In each of his next three at-bats, he homered on the first pitch. He had four homers in his last four swings of the Series.
- Set an individual record for most home runs in one Series (5), even though the Series went only six games.
- Became the first man ever to hit three homers in a Series in consecutive at-bats.
- Set a record for most total bases in one Series (25).
- Tied a record with 12 total bases in one game.
- Tied a record by scoring four runs in one game.

Jackson also finished with the highest Series batting average (.450), going 9 for 20.

Thurman Munson

4
The Hitters

Two years earlier, Munson was named captain. It didn't sound like much, but there had been no captain on the Yankees since the immortal Lou Gehrig. And that was many years before. He was made captain in 1976, a title he liked. He was looked up to by other players. He was the leader. George Steinbrenner likes leaders. He saw one in Thurman Munson. Steinbrenner suggested to Billy Martin that Munson should be made the captain. It was a great honor and he was happy with its meaning.

The happiness lasted only one season. The following year Reggie Jackson became a Yankee, and the unhappiness that engulfed Munson began. Suddenly, he didn't like the owner anymore. He became sullen. He felt he had been lied to. He wanted to be traded, wanted more money. It was a matter of principle to him. Steinbrenner had told him that

next to Catfish Hunter, he was the most highly paid Yankee. It wasn't so. Jackson was. He felt betrayed.

The 1977 season was perhaps Munson's most difficult in his eight years with the Yankees. Although it didn't affect his playing, it rubbed his personality. He talked with a bitterness in his voice. He was happy only when he was playing. He hit .308, with 18 home runs and 100 runs batted in. It was the third straight year that he had hit .300 and knocked in at least 100 runs. That's how important Munson was to the Yankees.

But his distrust of Steinbrenner and his dislike of Jackson upset his chemistry. Despite the fact that the Yankees won the World Series that year, Munson wanted to leave the club. He asked, practically demanded, that he be traded to a team closer to his home in Canton, Ohio, preferably the

Thurman Munson, 1976

(Top) Thurman Munson; (Bottom) Bucky Dent

Cleveland Indians. He barely enjoyed the satisfaction of winning the Series before making his feelings known.

Steinbrenner wasn't anxious to unload Munson. He realized how valuable he was, not only with his bat but also behind the plate. So, grudgingly, Munson returned to his ninth Yankee spring. He arrived a week late but had been given permission to do so in order to take care of his growing business interests around Canton.

The spring sun didn't thaw Munson's icy feelings. He maintained his unhappiness in not being traded. His displeasure was further emphasized when he decided he wasn't talking to reporters anymore. He was tired of all that had been written last season about him, Steinbrenner, and Jackson. He was determined to avoid a recurrence. He felt that not talking about it would greatly diminish its importance.

Graig Nettles shed some light on Munson's feelings regarding the press.

"I think that Thurman worried about what the other guys in the team will think about him," offered Nettles. "We all think about that. And some of it probably goes back to his unhappiness at not going to Cleveland in a trade."

Sometime in July Munson emerged from his shell of silence. He disclosed that he had worked out a new contract with Steinbrenner that would go through the 1981 season with a substantial raise in his income that would bring him to Jackson's level.

"It was satisfactory, the way it should have been before I was disgraced for two years," said Munson about his contract. "In that respect it satisfies me financially, but it doesn't help my attitude. Are material things supposed to help a guy who has had all these things eating at him for two years?

"I don't think my attitude has affected my play. But if you have the competitive spirit taken out of you, it's a tough game to play. Competitive spirit is mental. I just go out and play, but it's made me tired."

Unknown to many, Munson played in pain all season. He never complained. He had an ailing shoulder and a cyst behind his knee,

besides an assortment of bumps and bruises that are a catcher's way of life. When the pain was intense, Munson would play the outfield.

Munson learned to endure the pain. It even hurt his shoulder when he swung the bat—so much so that his power was diminished. He hit .297, but he produced only six home runs and drove in only 70 runs, far below his power efficiency of the previous three years. It was as noticeable as his unhappiness.

Lou Piniella was cast in the role of peacemaker in the Steinbrenner-Jackson-Munson scenario throughout most of the 1977 season. A humorous individual, Piniella kept the clubhouse loose. He often kidded his teammates in a likable way. But before the 1978 campaign began, Piniella shed his peacemaker role.

"Never again," exclaimed Piniella. "Last year there was a lot of stubbornness around. Nobody wanted to give in to anybody else. I don't say I was the chief peacemaker, but I tried to stay in between and smooth things out. To me, that seemed better than not getting involved at all. I was friendly with all the parties concerned, and we were dealing with grown men. But by the end of the year I was exhausted. I can't go through that again."

Piniella played a big part in the 1977 pennant drive. From August 10 until the end of the season, he batted .342, finishing with a .330 average. It was a strong finish for the 34-year-old veteran.

Once again in 1978 Piniella was expected to share the leftfield duties with Roy White. But when Lemon took over the team on July 25, he decided to change the situation. He wanted to play Piniella regularly.

"You're going to be an everyday player," said Lemon to Piniella one day in his office. "I want you to be a regular until you play your way out of the lineup."

At the time, Piniella was batting .304 with 30 runs batted in. He finished the season hitting .314 and drove in 69 runs. Again, he was a factor in the Yankees' pennant drive.

"Piniella has been super," exclaimed

Lou Piniella

Lemon. "I hoped he would come through when I made him a regular, but he has done better than I hoped he would."

Piniella looks at hitting as an art. He constantly works at it. He's been known to wake up in the middle of the night and experiment with his stance.

"I would say that he works on hitting, knows more about it than anybody I ever knew or ever played with," revealed Catfish Hunter. "I think he's one of the best line drive hitters in baseball. To me, he could play another four or five years. He's better now than he's ever been, I think. He knows the pitchers and knows how to hit, knows what to do."

Besides studying hitting, Piniella has a strange way of psyching himself up to do it. He does so by getting mad at himself.

"I just feel that to get the most out of myself I have to get up," explained Piniella. "Sometimes that means getting mad at myself. It makes me bear down harder. A lot of people, when I blow my stack, think I lose my concentration. Bull. That's why late in the game I'm usually a much better hitter, particularly when early in the game I've had bad times at bat."

One who had many bad times at bat was Mickey Rivers. It was completely unexpected. In 1977 Rivers batted .326, which was even better than the .312 he hit his first year with the Yanks after being acquired in a trade with the California Angels.

Strangely, Rivers had reported to spring training in a happy mood. He had received an extension on his contract that included more money and some incentive clauses. He looked forward to having another good season in 1978.

Lou Piniella

Once the campaign started, Rivers couldn't seem to get untracked. He wasn't playing with the gusto he showed in his first two years with the Yanks, running, hitting, catching fly balls that appeared to be hits. It appeared that Rivers wasn't concentrating on his game.

In a May weekend series against the Royals in Kansas City, Rivers didn't play very well in the field. The Yanks lost two of the games, both of them by one run. Billy Martin, natu-rally, was upset. He decided to bench his speedy centerfielder.

"Six of my players came to me and said something had to be done about Rivers," explained Martin.

Rivers got upset. So much so that he said that he would rather be traded anywhere than sit on the bench while Paul Blair took his place.

"I got nothing against Paul; but if this is gonna go on, I'm gonna ask them to send me

Mickey Rivers

away," declared Rivers. "They don't respect me anyway. I got a sore leg. I told him that. I also told him I would play the best I could.

"When he sits anybody else down, he calls them into his office. Why don't I get the same respect? He never called me in. I'm a person like everybody else. I don't want any privileges, but I shouldn't be treated differently."

By the middle of July, Rivers' batting average was in the .250 area, and he had only 10 stolen bases. A sensitive person, he seemed disturbed, quite possibly because his closest friend, Ken Holtzman, had been traded the previous month. He felt victimized.

"None of the guys want to be bothered by the front office," said Rivers. "We don't want to hear their problems on why we're not winning. We know why we're not winning, because other teams are playing better than us. Don't tell us more than we want to know."

(Above) Graig Nettles; (Opposite) Chris Chambliss, 1976

Everybody wanted to know what was wrong with Rivers. Later in the season he was fined twice by Bob Lemon for reporting to the ballpark late and once was reprimanded for his lackadaisical play. Rivers finished the season with only a .264 average. He was a victim of his own moods.

One who displayed an even temperament throughout all the turbulence that surrounded the club was Graig Nettles. He admitted being a bit unhappy following the 1977 season after leading the Yanks in homers with 37 and knocking in 107 runs. A one-year extension of his contract that would pay him close to $200,000 for the 1979 season made him feel content.

"I was unhappy last year, but things worked out," said Nettles. "I'm happy now."

In his first five years with the Yankees, the durable Nettles missed only 22 games. In his last two years Nettles belted 69 home runs and drove in 200 runs. But his value was also on the field, where he is considered the premier third baseman in the American League. Even Al Rosen, a former third baseman himself, marvels at Nettles' fielding.

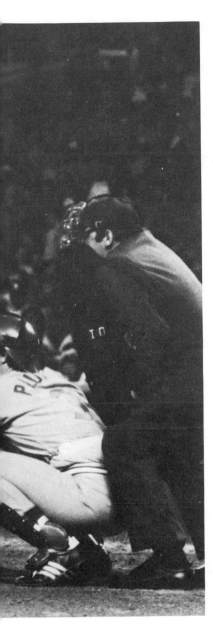

Roy White

"He's the best in the business, there's no doubt about it," beamed Rosen. "I'm not saying that just because he's a Yankee. Ask most baseball people. There are many outstanding third basemen—Mike Schmidt, George Brett, many others. All around, Nettles is the best. Year after year he produces, makes the big plays.

"I'm amazed at his quickness. He has a great body. Very supple, and seemingly can play for a long time. He gets to the ball faster than any third baseman I have ever seen. He has a great ability to dive for the ball and

recover. His agility is something that is outstanding."

Despite his easy going way, Nettles has a quick wit. It would bring smiles around the clubhouse. Like when Lyle, one of his best friends, was almost forgotten in the bullpen, Nettles said, "Sparky went from Cy Young to Sayonara in one year."

Even the turmoil that was the Yankees didn't affect him.

"So many kids dream of growing up to be ball players," said Nettles. "Others want to run away with the circus. I feel lucky. I got to do both."

Lemon, who observed Nettles for only half a season, had a great amount of admiration for the third baseman. He realized what a stabilizing influence Nettles was.

"No matter how he's hitting, it never affects his fielding," pointed out Lemon. "And when he gets hot, he can practically carry a ball club. He's never real high or never real low, almost even keel all the time. You just write him in on your lineup card and forget about him. You know you're not going to be hurting there."

In a sense, Nettles is a pitcher's best friend. He can beat the other team either with his glove or with his bat. But it is his glove that draws the most raves.

"A lot of people ask me if I work on my diving," replied Nettles. "That's something you can't work on. It has to be instinctive to do it because the first time you practice it, you'll probably fracture your shoulder. If you practice, it's not the same intensity as in a game. You have too much time to think about it. When I dive for a ball, very rarely do I feel myself hit the ground because there are so many things going through my mind. Therefore, it doesn't hurt.

"But if I was to try it in practice, I know I would be thinking about myself hitting the ground and there would be a terrible thud. But when I dive in a game, often halfway through the dive I know I'm going to get the ball; and before I hit the ground I'm thinking about getting up and making the throw."

Like Nettles, Chris Chambliss is another

Thurman Munson, 1977

quiet individual. So much so that often it's hard to detect that he's around. Like Nettles, he is a steady player, both at bat and on the field.

"I have no desire to outdo anybody in the press," emphasized Chambliss. "There's no reason. That's not what I'm here for."

Quietly and effectively, Chambliss goes about his duties. His only bad season was in 1974 after the Yankees got him from Cleveland. He was pressing and hit only .243. But after that, he showed his consistency by driving in 90 runs or more for the last three years.

"Every time I go up thinking home run,

that's when I'm in trouble," disclosed Chambliss. "Every home run I've had is when I'm up there just concentrating on making good contact. At the same time, a homer is the ultimate you can do as a ball player. You can't do any better. So when it happens, you know you've done the right thing."

The right thing for the Yankees to do was win the way they were expected to. Willie Randolph and Bucky Dent, the middle of the infield, were hurt at times. That made it difficult. But they returned and made it happen. So did Roy White, the veteran leftfielder who had a slow start but came on strong at the end. And in the end, the Yanks won . . .

5

Ron Guidry

He was down. He didn't want any part of baseball any longer. All he wanted was to go back home to Lafayette, Louisiana. There he could be alone and hunt and forget all about baseball. These were his boyhood dreams once again. He didn't think about pitching in the major leagues anymore. He had had his chance, although a brief one. Now he was ordered to go back to the minors, to Syracuse, and pitch some more. He was upset. He didn't want any part of Syracuse and the minors. Instead, he decided to quit. So Ron Guidry packed his car, and with his wife, Bonnie, at his side, began the long drive back to Lafayette from their New Jersey home.

It was still summertime. Maybe the fishing would be good. If anything, the peace and tranquility of the Louisiana countryside would allow him to think. Bonnie hardly spoke a word to her husband as they headed south. She knew him well. She knew he had

to think, and for a couple of hours she let him drive practically in silence. Then she finally began to talk.

"Do you really want to quit?" she began.

"I'm 25–26, and I have to get into something to make a living," he answered.

"This up-and-just-quitting is a first for you," she pointed out. "You know you really won't be happy not playing ball. Don't do something you'll regret the rest of your life."

"I'm getting too old to be going up and down," remarked Guidry.

"If you quit now, you'll never know," she added.

"Well, if you're willing to give it one more try, I will," he snapped.

She agreed. That was all the conversation needed. There wasn't any soul-searching or meditation, just an honest conversation between a man and his wife that put it all into perspective. Within the next few minutes,

Guidry turned his car around on Route 80 and headed for Syracuse, where he finished the 1976 season.

Guidry's determination showed. He had an outstanding year, or what was left of it, at Syracuse. His record didn't go unnoticed. He was 5–1 with an eye popping 0.68 earned run average. Still, one Yankee official confided to Guidry that he would have a better chance of making the team in 1977 if he pitched winter ball in the Caribbean League. He would have done so except for one important fact. His wife was expected to give birth to their first child, and he wanted to remain at home with her.

So, when Guidry reported to the Yankees for spring training, he was the father of a baby girl. Actually, it was the Yanks' third look at him. He was on the spring roster in 1975 and 1976 but never made it through the regular season. For a while he remained with the team in 1976. He started the year as the number two left-handed reliever behind Sparky Lyle. However, he was sent down to Syracuse before being called back and appeared in a few games. Then he sat. He sat for 61 days without pitching to a single batter. It was then that the Yankees decided to send Guidry back to Syracuse so that he could get some work.

"They said that I was not pitching enough," recalled Guidry. "That's when I got fed up. I decided that was it. I had had it. I felt I didn't have anything to prove to anybody by going back to Triple A. I thought if this is how highly they think of me, then I'm not going to go through this again.

"All told, I spent about a year with the big club; and I never got a chance to pitch. It was a mental defeat. But all that time I just didn't sit there and say, 'Well, I'll just sit and not do anything and collect.'

"Instead, I asked a couple of guys for some help. Every day that I would throw in the bullpen, I would ask Sparky how to grip the slider. He said, 'It's not so much how you grip it, it's what you do when you release it.'

"When you get to the point where you want to let your fastball go, you come down farther and hold it. Bring the ball down, and at the last moment, you yank it down. That gives it the downward motion. It's like pulling down a window shade."

Yet, during the spring of 1977, Guidry must have been thinking about Syracuse all over again. He did not have a good spring. Far from it. He appeared in six games and had an inflated earned run average of 10.24. Horrendous, to say the least. It was bad enough for owner George Steinbrenner and manager Billy Martin to agree to send him back to Syracuse again.

But Gabe Paul, the Yankees' president at the time, got them to hold off awhile. Paul demonstrated a bit more patience. He realized that Guidry had been sick during the winter and really wasn't strong enough for the rigors of spring training. To begin with, Guidry is only 5'9" and weighs 155 pounds. Imagine how a hot Florida sun can weaken him if he wasn't that healthy from the start.

"His problem that spring was that he still thought he had the kind of stuff where he could run the ball by everybody at the belt," disclosed pitcher Dick Tidrow. "Up here I haven't seen anybody who can consistently pitch at the belt.

"I just told him that I thought he'd see a lot of improvement if he started getting them across at the knees. After the hitters see that, then you can come up. Once he learned that slider and put these other things into perspective, that's when he started to become the pitcher we all knew he'd be."

Instead of Syracuse as first was feared, Guidry remained. It certainly wasn't because of what he showed in spring training. Rather, it was the faith that Paul had in him. Steinbrenner acknowledged it.

"I gave Gabe all the credit," he remarked. "He was the one who always thought that Guidry would make it."

Paul's persistence didn't weaken, although that spring he held his breath a few times.

"Sure, that spring made it tougher; but I never wavered in my position about keeping him," explained Paul. "He had been so fierce in the minor leagues, and you can't have this kind of arm and stuff and athletic ability and not make it."

Still, no one really knew what to expect of Guidry when the 1977 season opened. He was assigned to the bullpen once again as a back-up to Lyle. However, the Yankees' starting pitching rotation wasn't firmly established. Catfish Hunter had arm trouble; Ken Holtzman couldn't get it together; and Mike Torrez, who was acquired in a trade with the California Angels, was late in reporting to the club.

Martin turned to the still unknown Guidry and told him he would start against the Seattle Mariners on April 29. Calmly, Guidry went out and pitched a 3–0 shutout. His stock immediately soared.

"That was the first game where I really felt I had my good slider," remembered Guidry. "Guys started hacking at it and swinging and shaking their heads. It caught so many people by surprise.

"I showed them a guy they almost wanted to get rid of was somebody who could pitch if he got a chance to throw. There were a lot of people at the beginning of the season who didn't think I was going to be here.

"Billy Martin said I was terrible in spring training. I thought I was awful. My wife had a baby, and I had a lot of things to do so I didn't even go outside and throw a ball against the wall."

His first start in the majors was all that Guidry needed. He finished his first full season in the majors with a fine 16–7 record that included a 2.83 ERA, a win in the playoffs, and another in the World Series. His victory in the World Series was the high point of the season. He defeated the Los Angeles Dodgers, 4–2, on a four-hitter that gave the Yankees a 3–1 lead. It felt like just another game to him.

"I don't know what pressure is," he replied. "Maybe if I had been through it before, knew what it is, I might feel the pressure. But this was just another big game. Actually, I only get nervous when I'm hunting. You might shoot yourself in the foot."

There was a time not too long ago when Guidry thought his budding baseball career had come to an abrupt end. While still a sophomore at the University of Southwestern Louisiana, he played summer ball in Kansas. He wanted another pitch and began to experiment with a slider and hurt his arm. It was the most pain that Guidry had ever experienced.

"In 1970, I couldn't throw a ball 15 feet," revealed Guidry. "They told me that time was the only way to heal it."

By 1971, Guidry was back throwing a baseball. He played in a semi-pro league exhibition in New Orleans that baseball scouts kept an eye on. Guidry showed enough promise to be selected by the Yankees in the third round of the free agent draft. Yet, after four years in the minors, Guidry's record was only 13–16, hardly inspiring statistics. That's probably why the Yankees were so hesitant about him and why he made so many trips back and forth to Syracuse for two years.

"I hated to be used as a mop-up pitcher back then," disclosed Guidry. "But I became more confident every time I went up. Once I knew what the job called for, I did well. You have to do something to catch their eye, but I was never given the chance. You have to be in the right spot at the right time. If you get a break, you have to capitalize on it."

Did he ever. After his solid 1977 season in which he got his chance and made the most of it, Guidry established himself as a starter before the 1978 campaign began. By now, everyone was wondering how such a small pitcher could throw such a big fastball. His fastball was clocked at 92 miles an hour, which is among the fastest in the game. He also mastered a hard slider which is fired at almost the same velocity as his fastball. It's no wonder that hitters are confused and often strike out.

Like the night in Yankee Stadium in 1978. It was still early in the season, June 17, and the Yankees were playing the California Angels. Although the season was two months old, the Yanks were still struggling, playing barely above the .500 mark. By the time the game was over, Guidry shattered a 59-year-old team record by striking out 18 Angels, the highest ever by a left-hander in league history, in spinning a four-hit, 4–0 shutout. In one word, Guidry was simply awesome.

It was the greatest individual effort of his brief career. He was in total command of the hitters throughout the entire game. His fastball was popping and his slider was snapping, and the Angels were swinging off balance to the rhythmic chanting of the crowd. The Angel batters were winding up and chopping down in a futile effort to make contact with one of Guidry's pitches. It never happened.

Even the Angel players were awed by Guidry's performance. It's not likely that they will see one like it again. At least, they hope not. Nolan Ryan, who is acknowledged to throw the fastest ball in the major leagues, admired Guidry's effort.

"The kid was simply overpowering," exclaimed Ryan. "The entire bench was laughing because we felt we were overmatched."

His teammate, Joe Rudi, couldn't disagree with that assessment. Rudi, a right-handed hitter, struck out all four times he faced Guidry.

"If you saw that pitching too often, there would be a lot of guys doing different jobs," concluded Rudi.

Umpire Ted Hendry got a full view of Guidry's fastballs. He was the plate umpire and watched the ball all the way until it reached catcher Thurman Munson's glove.

"His ball was exploding," remarked Hendry.

Tidrow got a warm feeling of satisfaction in watching Guidry's masterpiece. Like Ryan, he saw it from a pitcher's eye.

"They were choking up on the bat, swinging defensively, just trying to meet the ball and couldn't do it," smiled Tidrow.

Amazingly, Guidry took his record-breaking performance in stride. He was as calm as could be. He's that way. He is not affected or overwhelmed by sudden fame or attention. It's all part of the game to him, and he is not surprised by what takes place.

"I really don't have a pattern of pitching where I say to myself, 'I'm gonna throw a fastball away, a fastball in, a slider away, and a slider in,'" explained Guidry quite surprisingly. "Usually my ball is so alive that it's not gonna do what I want. I just try to throw it as hard as I can in the general vicinity of the catcher's target.

"I still think I'm a pitcher, not a thrower, because I know where I want to throw it. But when you start thinking too much about throwing the ball here and there, you go back to becoming a finesse pitcher. Right now that's not the type of pitcher I am. I could become that way if somebody were to say to me: 'Okay, we're gonna take six miles away from your fastball.'

"But right now, with the velocity I have, I can make mistakes and get away with pitches that other guys can't, so I'm gonna continue that way. In my mind, when I don't have the good stuff anymore, all I gotta say to myself is, 'Ron, you gotta start pitching to spots, you gotta change up a little more.' I know I can do that now, and that's a bridge that every pitcher comes to.

"I'm always asked how can I throw so hard since I'm not all that big, and I have no answer for that question. All I know is that I have always been able to throw hard. I began playing Little League when I was eight years old. Even though the other kids were bigger, I could always throw harder than they could. It was the same thing in American Legion ball. I guess it's much the same today, even in this league.

"All that's happening on this club hasn't affected me. If you go about your job, nobody can say anything against you. The only time I feel something is when people refer to 'the team,' because I'm a part of this team. Whatever happens the rest of the year, I still say we have a good team. But I personally very seldom get into controversy.

"All the time I wasn't getting a chance to pitch, I just kept telling myself, 'Stay cool, don't get upset. When they give the ball to you, you'll be able to make a few people sorry they didn't try you before.'"

But they did give Guidry the ball regularly now. They even looked for him, counted on him like never before. And he was making a lot of other teams sorry that they had to face him. Ron Guidry with a baseball in his hands in 1978 was practically unbeatable. He won his first 13 games and finished the year-of-the-Yankee miracle with a 25–3 record! It was no wonder that he was the unanimous winner of the Cy Young Award.

Yet, Guidry did more, so much more. One has to go deeper, behind the wins, to see what a phenomenal season Guidry produced in 1978. It's entirely possible that it will never be duplicated. Guidry is credited with achievements like:

- Posting .893 winning percentage, the highest in baseball history by a 20-game winner.
- Striking out 18 California Angels on June 17 at Yankee Stadium to set a Yankee club record, and an A. L. record for most strike-outs in a 9-inning game by a left-hander.
- 248 strikeouts in the season, which tied him for third in the major leagues with Phil Niekro, behind J. R. Richard and Nolan Ryan (it was second in the A. L.—the 248 strikeouts broke the Yankee single-season record previously set by Jack Chesbro in 1904 with 239).

- His 9 shutouts, which tied Babe Ruth's A. L. record for most shutouts by a left-hander set in 1916.
- Leading the major leagues in wins (25), ERA (1.74), winning percentage (.893), and shut-outs (9).
- 15 of his 25 wins during the regular season following a Yankee loss, including his World Series win.
- Being named American League Player of the Month in June and September.
- His 1.74 ERA being the second lowest in history by an A. L. left-hander (second only to Dutch Leonard's 1.01 in 1914).
- His 1.74 ERA being the lowest by a left-hander since Sandy Koufax's 1.73 in 1966.
- Yanks winning 30 of the 35 games that Guidry started this year and scoring only 7 runs in the 5 they lost.

Ron Guidry and the Seagram "Oscar," October 25, 1978.

- Winning 33 of his last 37 regular season decisions; if you add his perfect 4–0 post season record, Ron has gone 37–4 since August 10, 1977.
- Winning 12 of his last 14 regular season decisions in 1978, including 7 shutouts; 3 of his last 5 wins being 2-hit shutouts.
- The American League batting .193 against Guidry this year, as opposed to .261 overall.
- Striking out 10 or more in a game 8 times.

at more than 90 miles an hour. Besides, throwing so many fastballs will only break down his arm eventually; and he doesn't want that to happen. So, while he developed a slider, he is thinking about developing still another pitch. Another weapon in his arsenal will only confuse American League hitters all the more.

"I'm going to have to develop something off-speed to complement my hard stuff,"

How Guidry Rates with Other Yankee Greats

	G	W	L	Pct.	IP	H	BB	SO	SH	ERA
Ron Guidry, 1978	35	25	3	.893	273.2	187	72	248	9	1.74
Mel Stottlemyre, 1965	37	20	9	.690	291	250	88	155	4	2.63
Whitey Ford, 1961	39	25	4	.862	283	242	92	209	3	3.21
Allie Reynolds, 1952	35	20	8	.714	244	194	97	160	6	2.06
Vic Raschi, 1950	33	21	8	.724	257	232	116	155	2	4.00
Spud Chandler, 1943	30	20	4	.833	253	197	54	134	5	1.64
Ernie Bonham, 1942	28	21	5	.808	226	199	24	71	6	2.27
Red Ruffing, 1939	28	21	7	.750	233	211	75	95	4	2.93
Lefty Gomez, 1934	38	26	5	.839	282	223	96	158	6	2.33
Waite Hoyt, 1928	42	23	7	.767	273	279	60	67	3	3.36
Bullet Joe Bush, 1922	39	26	7	.788	255	240	85	92	0	3.31
Carl Mays, 1921	49	27	9	.750	337	332	76	70	1	3.05
Russ Ford, 1910	36	26	6	.813	300	194	70	209	8	1.65
Jack Chesbro, 1904	55	41	13	.759	455	338	88	239	6	1.82

"I'm surprised that my record was so great, but I wasn't surprised by the way I pitched," said Guidry. "I always thought I could pitch that way. I could have lost 10 or 12 games I won. I was fortunate to pitch a lot of good games when we were struggling. The club and I worked pretty well together. It was a great season, a season a lot of pitchers dream about.

"I always wondered what it would be like to have a year like I had. Now, even if I never have another year like it, I'll be able to say that in 1978 I was the best. People will remember the year Guidry and the Yankees had in 1978. It will be hard to repeat. If I lose four games, people are going to say I'm on the decline, I'm all washed up. I know that seasons like mine come along just once in a long while."

Yet, Guidry is thinking ahead. Far down the road. He, more than anyone else, realizes that his fastball won't continually be clocked

disclosed Guidry. "I've got to learn not to throw so hard, so often. If I continue throwing with so much velocity, my career won't be as long. I couldn't afford to try something different in 1977. I experimented with a change-up occasionally, but I didn't have one hundred percent confidence in it. But now I'm ready to try it out to prolong my career."

Guidry thought seriously about developing a change-up after the third game of the 1978 World Series. After the Yankees lost the first two games to the Los Angeles Dodgers, Guidry threw enough fastballs on the way to a 5–1 victory.

A day later, there was a story circulating that Guidry's arm had given out and that he wouldn't be able to pitch against the Dodgers if the Series went seven games. Actually, what Guidry had said was misunderstood. Still, it created some excitement.

"After the third game of the Series I told

someone that my arm was tired and sore," explained Guidry. "What I meant was that it was tired and sore from that game. After nine innings it had a right to be. It was misinterpreted.

"I decided to let the Dodgers think I'm tired. If they think that and then all of a sudden I uncork a pitch about 95 miles an hour, it might shake them up. I would have been ready to pitch the seventh game, if necessary. My arm felt good."

Guidry's resiliency is extraordinary for such a small pitcher. He is a natural athlete who doesn't have to participate in any training programs to stay in shape. His biggest interest in the off-season is going hunting, and he does that whenever he can. At heart he is a country boy. He still remembers his first impression of New York.

"When I first saw it, I really didn't say anything," he recalled. "I just shook my head. It was immense. I guess when you're just a country fella, you can't say anything about it.

"I'm used to green trees and open space. This was amazing, and I still have the same impression. It's a hurry, hurry atmosphere. If you have to go two blocks, sprint it. I just can't get over it."

What some baseball observers can't get over is the time it took Guidry to develop. Birdie Tebbetts, a former catcher and major league manager who works as a special assignment scout for the Yankess, explained it.

"You never know," began Tebbetts. "Maybe the fact that he didn't get a chance to pitch immediately was the best thing that ever happened to him. You have to grow into greatness; it just doesn't come overnight.

"I think that perhaps there is an admission price that you have to pay to be a great ball player. No pitcher that I know of has ever come up who hasn't at some time in his career had to pay the price of being great. It either happens early or in the middle of your career, and you're going to have to adjust to it if you're going to be great.

"When Guidry was a young kid, he hurt his arm. That was part of his admission price. He had to sit by and see great pitchers pitch when he was wanting to pitch so badly that he could taste it. In our game, no matter what anybody thinks or what is written or said, everyone has to pay the admission price. I think Ron Guidry has now paid his. But if he has to pay the price again, he can adapt to it very easily.

"In the years since I've been around, Guidry is the only guy who made me think immediately of Lefty Gomez. He had about the same kind of body, the same kind of delivery and a chance at the same kind of stuff. Everyone in the organization thought Guidry was going to be some kind of pitcher."

At least manager Bob Lemon thinks so. Lemon, a Hall of Famer, was some kind of a pitcher himself with the Cleveland Indians. He was a 20-game winner seven times. Not many pitchers can match that record. He has a special admiration for Guidry.

"Anybody with that kind of stuff has to amaze you," remarked Lemon. "He's as fast or faster than Bob Feller and Hal Newhouser in their heyday. He's probably the smallest fellow I've seen who can generate that type of heat for so long. He makes you nervous when he walks somebody or gives up a hit. You think it's a rally."

That's how much faith the Yankees as a whole have in Guidry. When the club needed a win in 1978, they looked to Guidry and he came through. He started 35 games, and the Yankees won 30 of them. More important, 15 of his 25 wins came after the Yanks had lost. He clearly established himself as the stopper. That's how much they depended on Guidry.

"I don't view my role on the staff as a burden," disclosed Guidry. "I think it's a compliment. I always knew I could pitch. I don't feel there is any great pressure on me. I don't feel like I have to win.

"If I pitch as well as I can and try as hard as I can, most of the time I'm gonna come out on top. If you go back and look at the records of all the great pitchers, you'll see they pitched many bad games. I'm not gonna be any different. I know that somewhere along

the line I'm gonna get my butt kicked all over the place. You've got to accept defeat. I guess that's what makes me different. I know it's gonna come."

It is hard to picture defeat after Guidry's first two full years with the Yankees. During that time, he has a 41–10 record. There is no pitcher in baseball who can come close to matching those credentials. It is the stuff that greatness is made of, and it begins with Cy Young Awards.

Yet, the magnitude of the award hasn't been fully absorbed by Guidry. He's pure country. He doesn't place himself above anyone else. He'd much rather contribute to another championship. And if a Cy Young Award goes along with it, all well and good.

"It's a great honor to win it, but it will mean more once I'm out of baseball when I reflect on the past," explained Guidry. "I'll be able to say, if it ever happens again, that in 1978 I won the Cy Young Award, signifying that I was the best pitcher.

"But I want to be on a championship Yankee team again. Even if I win just 15 games, as long as I contribute, I'll be satisfied."

The great ones won't stop at 15 . . .

6

The Pitchers

On paper it looked like the best pitching staff that money could buy. Long before the 1978 season began, the Yankees had the look of a million-dollar pitching staff. Through the free agent market, the Yankees acquired three hurlers that gave them that look. One was Rich Gossage, the National League's top reliever; another was Rawly Eastwick, who was the best reliever the Cincinnati Reds had. The third was Andy Messersmith, who was looked upon as a starter. In the Yankees' winter book, the staff was deep. Messersmith was figured to join a starting rotation that included Ron Guidry, Catfish Hunter, Don Gullett, Ed Figueroa, and possibly even Dick Tidrow. Gossage was expected to join Sparky Lyle in short relief while Eastwick was figured to be the long relief man along with one of the younger hurlers like Jim Beattie or Ken Clay.

It didn't work out as expected. The million-dollar staff became a million-dollar hospital bill. Gullett and Messersmith had arm trouble that sidelined them for the year. Hunter also had arm miseries but doggedly hung on in an effort to work out the problem. Figueroa also experienced some minor malady that hampered his pitching. In the early months of the season, only Guidry was healthy and winning.

The Yankees were looking for a big year from Hunter. In 1977 arm trouble accounted for a very mediocre 9–9 season, one in which he pitched only 143 innings. Yet, when he reported to spring training, he still was beset with doubts about his arm, which began bothering him late in the 1975 season.

"I feel like I'm getting back to 100 percent," said Hunter the first week into the 1978 season. "I hope I can keep on going. I felt at the end of spring training that I was on the way back because it didn't hurt me to throw. I think the shoulder problem will work its way out. I hope it comes around so I can go more than six or seven innings. But as long as we have Sparky and Gossage in the bullpen, maybe we're better off in my coming out early. You know, this is the first year I ever asked to be taken out. In past years I didn't want to come out if I was dying."

The Yanks desperately needed a healthy Hunter after Gullett and Messersmith were shelved with injuries. But Hunter himself wasn't all that healthy. He had a 2–3 record but couldn't finish a game because his shoulder would stiffen up in the late innings. The Yanks felt that a rest would help cure his shoulder and put Hunter on the disabled list.

Near the end of June, Hunter came off the disabled list. Martin asked him to pitch one inning in relief against the Red Sox. It was his first such outing in a regular season game since 1972. But Hunter and the Yanks had to find out how his arm was.

It didn't look good. Hunter yielded two king-size home runs, two other hits, and a walk in his one-inning appearance. He couldn't explain it.

"I don't know what happened to my arm," said Hunter. "It's gone south. If my arm felt good, I could win 20 games easy."

What the Yanks had to do was to put Hunter on the disabled list again. It appeared that he was finished for the season. His condition was a very serious blow to the Yanks' pennant hopes.

Four days after his painful appearance against the Red Sox, Hunter took his ailing arm to Dr. Maurice Cowen. Hunter's arm hurt so badly that he could hardly move it. Cowen had helped Gullett earlier by manipulating his arm and shoulder. So, Cowen put Hunter to sleep and began working on his arm.

"He grabbed my right arm and bent it back 45 degrees," explained Hunter later. "Straight back. He told me later that when he got it way back, something in the arm popped. He said it popped so loud he thought he broke my arm. They don't know what happens. All they know is that it breaks the adhesions loose in the arm."

Whatever Cowen did worked. Hunter be-

gan to pitch like the Catfish of old. Like the time from 1971 to 1975 when he won at least 20 games each year. First he hurled eight shutout innings against the Texas Rangers. Then five days later he went against the Baltimore Orioles and pitched a 3–0 shutout. It was his first complete game since August 25, 1977. More encouraging was the fact that he didn't feel any pain in his shoulder.

"The best thing is that my shoulder didn't hurt," exclaimed Hunter. "I feel like I can do what I want now, throw the ball to spots, put the ball where I want it. It makes me feel good to help this team for a change. I believe control is the name of the game as far as pitching is concerned. If I can put the ball where I want it, when I want, then I can be effective."

The Cat was indeed effective. He was back from a battle with diabetes, an 0–2 beginning, and two trips to the disabled list. In the month of August, Hunter won all six games he pitched. The Yankees were alive again. They needed Hunter's arm.

"Maybe I'm making up for it now," beamed Hunter. "It's hard to believe one treatment helped me that much. At least I can throw strikes with no pain."

Since he got off the disabled list, Hunter gave the Yanks a lift the rest of the season. He won ten and lost only three. He reduced his ERA from a bulging 6.51 to 3.58, finishing with a 12–6 record. Without his comeback, the Yanks wouldn't have been able to overtake the Red Sox.

"It feels good to contribute something to the ball club instead of sitting on the bench and knowing you can't do anything," said Hunter. "There were times I thought the arm would hurt forever. It's great to show 'em you can win again rather than get your brains beat out every night.

"I always thought something would happen, and I'd come back and pitch. I knew there had to be a doctor somewhere who could help. I would have kept on trying as long as my contract ran because I know if my arm comes around and I can throw, I can win easily. I still had my control. It isn't something you forget. It's like riding a bicycle. All you need is to get back on, and you remember how it's done.

"When I go out there now, I feel I know what I'm doing. There's no pain at all, and I know I can get the ball where I want it. Earlier this year, no way I thought I'd be back if it got this far down the road. I thought in September they'd say, 'Go on home. No way you can pitch. We're bringing up another guy to take your spot.'"

The one spot the Yankees felt they needed additional help in was the bullpen. When they had a chance to get Gossage, they went all out. He was a hard-throwing right-hander who threw the strikeout pitch. Gossage had

Catfish Hunter, 1976

(Opposite) Rich Gossage; (Above) Don Gullett

won 11 games, saved 26, and put together a 1.62 earned run average in 72 games for the Pittsburgh Pirates in 1977. His fastball had struck out 151 batters in 131 innings. He was an expensive goose. He cost the Yankees $3.6 million for six years.

"I think this is a great business deal considering the anticipated return," replied Steinbrenner. "I made the best business deal, period."

The signing of Gossage raised some eyebrows. What would the Yankees want with another bullpen ace when they already had Sparky Lyle, the 1977 Cy Young Award winner? But the Yanks saw an opportunity to strengthen their bullpen and didn't hesitate in the least.

"I've heard so much about Sparky that I just can't wait to get together with him," said Gossage. "Everybody says that he's a good man and a real riot. A team needs a guy like him. There's plenty of work for all of us. Sparky will see. There won't be any trouble

at all. I'll pitch and he'll pitch, and we'll all do fine.

"I loved last year. I felt great. I had my fastball going and my slider and a change-up, and I'd come in and blow the ball past guys. I want to be ready this season again. I figure I can have the same type of year that I had last season. And that was a whole lot of fun."

Still, when the Yanks assembled for spring training, the speculation centered around Gossage and Lyle. Most observers couldn't see how they both could be used effectively. Both Gossage and Lyle were the type of pitchers that had to be used often to be effective.

"I just know Sparky and I will get our work," repeated Gossage. "If this was a football season, we'd be in trouble. But it's a long season. I don't know how Martin is going to work it, but I can guess. Once a starter gets in trouble, he's going to be gone. Billy is going to turn it over to one of us or both of us."

There is certainly nothing wrong with a lefty-righty combination. That's what Martin was thinking about. He remembered the great Cleveland Indian bullpen of a few years back that featured Don Mossi, a left-hander, and Ray Narleski, a right-hander.

"Sparky is going to work as much as he did last year," claimed Martin. "Maybe more. Suppose I go with Gullett and take him out in the sixth inning. The other team is going to have a right-handed lineup at that point, so I come in with Gossage. Now they switch to left-handed hitters, and I've got Lyle. Lots of times they might work the same game."

Gullett understood. He saw the same situation when he was with Cincinnati. And it worked quite effectively.

"When you've got a bullpen like we've got, you can afford to pull your starters early," pointed out Gullett. "What you also have to remember is that most of us are on multi-year contracts and that we don't have to impress with complete games or great statistics to get our money next year. That's a key. But the biggest key of all is winning games. If our bullpen is making sure that the team is winning, then the starters have no reason to complain. What makes it so great is that Billy has balance with the left-hander and the right-hander. He can use up a whole team's bench in two or three innings."

Martin didn't hesitate to use Gossage regularly once the season began. But strangely, Gossage was ineffective. He lost three games before he recorded his first win. Yet, he wasn't concerned. He was throwing hard even though he was getting beaten.

"The thing about me is that I can't alter myself," explained Gossage. "There are a lot of fastball-hitting teams, but I'm a fastball pitcher. It's strength against strength, and the battle goes to the stronger. When I'm right, the ball moves a lot. Good pitching can always beat good hitting."

As the season progressed, Gossage validated his argument. The strikeouts came and so did the saves, and he was a key factor during the Yankees' two-month surge to the top. At times he was totally overpowering, like the night in September when he struck out three Seattle batters on 11 pitches.

"I haven't been able to do that so much this year," revealed Gossage. "I felt better than I have all season. The pressure is there, the tension, but it's great. You can't smile while you're out there because you're so involved in what you're doing, but then you come in here and you just think how great it was. Then you smile."

Gossage finished his first year with the Yankees with a 9–10 record. But the numbers are deceiving. He appeared in 62 games, produced a 1.91 earned run average, struck out 120 batters in 132 innings, and led the league in saves with 26. He felt he should have done better.

"I'm disappointed," he exclaimed. "I think I could have done better. I should have had 29 or 30 saves by September. But it's taken me time to get my feet on the ground here. I wanted to do so good. I remember Opening Day here, the boos. We opened the season in Texas, and Richie Zisk beat me with a home run. Then I pitched in Milwaukee, and Larry Hisle hit a homer off me and we lost. We get home, and I go out there and get

booed. I was trying to impress everybody, but I was pressing instead."

Lyle didn't want to impress anybody. He didn't have to. He had been the Yankees' bullpen ace for five years. What he wanted was an explanation of his new status now that Gossage was added to the bullpen. He wanted assurance that he would work as much as he did in 1977 when he was 13–5 with 26 saves and had a 2.17 earned run average over 137 innings, a performance that earned him the Cy Young Award. Besides Gossage, the Yanks added Eastwick a week later, and Lyle felt that the bullpen was a bit crowded when he reported to spring training.

The prankish Lyle turned up in Ft. Lauderdale five days late. A practical joker, Lyle had the tables turned on him by Steinbrenner. When Lyle walked off the plane that afternoon, Steinbrenner arranged for a local high school band, complete with cheerleaders, to greet Lyle. It caught him by surprise.

"I don't believe this," exclaimed Lyle. "I just don't believe it. I couldn't have pulled a better one than this myself. If I had known about this, I would have stepped off the plane in a Red Sox uniform. I didn't know the Yankees were so happy to see me. I guess I owe George one. I'll think of something. The last time I saw George he was chewing a Reggie Bar."

But Lyle's happiness didn't last long. He met privately with Steinbrenner for the first time and told him that he was unhappy with the money he was getting. He also told him that he wanted to be traded, something he had mentioned earlier to club president Al Rosen and general manager Cedric Tallis.

"I reiterated my desire to be traded," disclosed Lyle. "We didn't discuss money, but that's what it boils down to. I want to go somewhere where I can get more money. I see what other pitchers on the staff are getting. That's why I want to get the hell out of here. Why shouldn't I go to another club and pitch the way I have for the Yankees and make more money? I want more than I'm getting."

Sparky Lyle

It was an unhappy spring for Lyle. Once the season began, he wasn't any happier. He met with Rosen, still seeking more money. He was told to sit tight. Brooding, Lyle didn't show up for a welcome-home Yankee lun-cheon and was fined $500. That added to his unhappiness.

Yet, during the first month of the season, Lyle appeared in 10 games. It was the same number of appearances he had made over the same time period last year. He registered five saves, which tied him for the league lead. Still, Lyle didn't find joy, not with a crowded bullpen and an unappreciative front office that refused to give him additional money.

"We've never renegotiated the contract," admitted Rosen. "Maybe he would find that I have a valid point. When a club signs a player to a long-term contract, it takes a risk that the player will perform at the same level and that he will be injury-free. He doesn't have to do anything except pitch. We don't have to do anything except watch him pitch."

It was obvious that Lyle wasn't going to get any more money. He was hoping that he would be traded. In fact, at one point, he was counting the days. His eye was on the June 15 trading deadline.

"Four more days and maybe I'll be out of here," fumed Lyle. "I'll go anywhere, even to Cleveland. I haven't thrown well all year, and I won't throw well all year. I'm just not getting enough work."

A month later, Lyle stormed off the mound at Yankee Stadium. It was the same night, July 17, that Reggie Jackson incurred his suspension. Lyle left after the sixth inning, fuming on his way to the clubhouse, "Get somebody else. I'm not a long relief man!"

"Sparky doesn't complain to me," said Martin. "I know he doesn't like long relief. He's told me, and I understand the way he feels. But I don't have a long relief man. I have to use him sometimes. Who knows? The next time I might come in with Gossage early and then look for Sparky."

With a strong second-half effort by Gossage, Lyle was used less. He wore a mask of unhappiness on his face. There was no question that it would be his last season as a Yankee. He finished with a 9–3 record with only nine saves and a high 3.47 ERA. He didn't even make a World Series appearance.

Jim Beattie

"My main attribute is my ability to get up for games mentally," declared Lyle. "It's not that I haven't been up, it's just that some of the edge is gone. I thrive on tough situations. I haven't been getting many; and when I have, I haven't always had it, physically or mentally."

Even Ed Figueroa wasn't happy with the pitching situation. At the beginning of the year, when the Yanks looked deep in pitchers, it appeared that Figueroa would get the chance to pitch only about once a week. He had set his sights on 20 wins, and the pitching rotation didn't please him. He even asked to be traded.

"I've been the Yanks' most consistent pitcher the two years I've been here," said Figueroa, alluding to his 35–21 record. "And I don't think I've been treated the right way. I would like to win 20 games this season. That's important to me. I think I should be able to do it this year.

"They can trade me away with all these pitchers they got. Gullett is coming back. Messersmith is coming back. I asked to be traded last year. I asked to be traded after the

Dick Tidrow

World Series. I asked my agent to talk to Al Rosen this year and to get me traded.

"They say no. They say they need me. Well, I don't want to pitch every seventh day. I want to pitch every fourth day. They can trade me. I know they can.

"I can't pitch every six-seven days. I get only one-two runs, lose the game; then I have to wait another six days before I pitch. At least if you lose a close game, you can always come back three or four days later and try again.

"I am 29 years old. I can pitch. I can pitch a lot more. I don't like this seven-day wait. I want to go to California."

Figueroa was also looking for more money. With the big money spent on the new hurlers, Figueroa figured there should be some for him, too.

"If they give me more money or if they don't, I will still do my best," claimed Figueroa. "I would like an adjustment. I think I deserve it. But I can't make them do anything. My job is to be a winner again."

And he was. After a slow start, the Puerto Rican right-hander got hot. In mid-July, Figueroa was only 8–7. In the last half of the season he realized his goal of winning 20 games, becoming the first Puerto Rican pitcher ever to do it. Figueroa won 12, lost two, had a 2.99 ERA, and finished with a 20–9 record.

The Yanks' deep pitching staff suddenly got thin in the early months of the season. Gullett and Messersmith were done for the year, Eastwick was traded, and Hunter was ailing. Suddenly, the situation was bleak.

However, the Yanks got some needed help from Dick Tidrow, who pitched long relief and started occasionally, and from rookie Jim Beattie. Between them they won 13 games. It turned out to be enough to complete the Yankee miracle . . .

Catfish Hunter

Spring training

7
1978 Season

It was supposed to be a happy spring. Billy Martin had grandiose dreams about winning two consecutive World Series; George Steinbrenner shared the same dreams, signing such high-priced free agents as pitchers Rich Gossage, Rawly Eastwick, and Andy Messersmith; and Reggie Jackson and Thurman Munson both expected to find peace and love. On paper, the Yankees appeared much stronger than in 1977 when they won their first World Championship since 1962. Certainly a great many experts figured it the same way. The Yankees were picked to repeat as American League champions with their strongest competition expected to come from the Boston Red Sox.

Martin couldn't wait for spring training to begin. In fact, months before the team was scheduled to report to its training base at Ft. Lauderdale, Florida, he sent each of his players a personal letter. It was a long letter, but Martin wanted to show that he meant busi-

ness and to put his players in a serious state of mind.

Despite the fact that Martin put it all down on paper, several of his players were in an unhappy mood when training camp opened. Sparky Lyle, for one, was quite disturbed that the Yanks had signed Gossage. In 1977 Lyle was voted the Cy Young Award as the best pitcher in the American League. He was upset by the realization that his role would be diminished through the addition of Gossage. Lyle was faced with the fact that he wouldn't be the team's number one reliever after having maintained that position for several seasons.

Jackson also was concerned. Although he had been the World Series hero just a few months before, none of his other teammates made him feel that he was part of the team. Being a sensitive individual, he was disturbed by the team's chilly attitude. He tried to overlook it, at least publicly, but down deep

(Left) Sparky Lyle

it bothered him. He felt his three-home-run explosion in the sixth game of the World Series against the Los Angeles Dodgers was unappreciated. It was as if it had never happened. Hardly any of the players ever made mention of it.

The off-season didn't appear to warm the feelings of some others. Munson still hoped that he would be traded. He desired to be sent to Cleveland so that he would be close to his home in Canton, Ohio. The sharp remarks that Jackson had made in a magazine article early last season still were fresh in his mind. He didn't want to endure another season like 1977 in which turmoil and unrest permeated the clubhouse. Munson was determined not to speak at any great length

Reggie Jackson, 1977

Spring training

Spring training

with reporters covering the team, preferring to remain silent if possible.

There were other grumblings, too. Ed Figueroa was still incensed at not being used at all in the World Series. Outfielders Roy White and Mickey Rivers also were brooding. White was upset by his limited play in the playoffs and the World Series and by the fact that the Yankees were looking for another leftfielder in the trade market. Rivers was testy about a new contract, one that would give him more money. So despite the fact that the Yankees opened training camp as the world champions, no one knew what to expect. Yet, those who had covered the ball club felt that it was inevitable that something would happen.

Martin was loose and happy. He was confident. He realized that he had a solid club, one that had an excellent chance to become world champions a second time. The addition of the new players certainly strengthened the club. All he had to do was prime them in the spring and then drive them toward the championship. That's all he wanted, that and togetherness. Most of the players were blasé about the togetherness. They just shrugged about it. After all, they were the world champions. And what's more, they were confident of repeating that success. The bottom line was winning, and that's what they were prepared to do.

The promise of spring suddenly turned shallow once the regular season began. The

(Right) Bucky Dent

Yankees didn't exactly tear up the exhibition season. Still, Martin wasn't concerned. He wanted a carefree training camp, and he had one. However, Steinbrenner showed some concern. He felt that the team didn't work hard enough and wasn't physically ready and couldn't care less about the mental aspect at this point in the season. He expressed his displeasure to Martin who reassured him that everything would be fine.

But it wasn't. The Yanks began slowly, too slowly even for Martin. During the first month of the season they played just about .500 baseball. That's not the way pennants are won. Actually, the Yanks' mediocre play was compounded by a series of injuries. Every other day someone had to withdraw from the lineup. That in itself was frustrating. Ailments suffered by Hunter and Messersmith thinned the starting rotation. Second baseman Willie Randolph, shortstop Bucky Dent, and centerfielder Mickey Rivers also were hampered by injuries most of the early months.

Even more frustrating was that some of the key players weren't productive. Jackson, Munson, and Rivers got off to slow starts which made the Yankee batting attack that much weaker. Gossage also had trouble in the beginning which further accented the loss of Hunter and Messersmith. With such an inauspicious start, the players' tempers started to mount. They boiled over in May.

The Yankees had just lost a tough 10–9 game to the Kansas City Royals in Kansas City, which left them with a 17–12 record. The win gave the Royals the series, 2–1, the other victory being a close 4–3 decision over the Yanks in the opening meeting of the three-game set. The finale was a game that Martin felt the Yanks should have won.

What made him seethe was Rivers' outfield play. He allowed one fly ball that appeared catchable to fall safely ten feet in front of him. Then in the bottom of the ninth inning, Rivers didn't come anywhere close to catching Amos Otis' game-winning double. By the time Martin reached the clubhouse, he was mad.

Mickey Rivers

Within a few minutes he grew even angrier. Walking through the clubhouse, he looked over at Rivers and saw him joking with Cliff Johnson.

"That's right, laugh it up on the bus, guys, keep on laughing," snapped Martin.

Before leaving Kansas City, Martin telephoned Yankee president Al Rosen. He was still upset and spoke to Rosen for close to a half-hour about the game.

"Billy was upset, and I can understand why he was," confirmed Rosen. "When he sees something on the field he feels is intolerable, he gets all welled up inside. He'll do everything he possibly can to win. He was that way as a ballplayer, and he's no different as a manager. He felt that Rivers could have done much more than he did against Kansas City."

When the Yankees boarded their plane for Chicago, Martin was still seething. Munson made a couple of visits to the lavatory in the first class section where Martin was sitting. However, before returning to his seat in the first row of the coach section, Munson stopped long enough to talk to Martin each time.

Munson realized that Martin was mad. In fact, he even told Gossage so. A short while later, Munson stood up in the rear of the first class section. Martin happened to turn around and see him.

"What's your argument?" asked Martin. "I don't have any argument with you. If you have an argument with me, you can meet me in my room."

Munson felt challenged. He shouted back to Martin; before anyone realized it, the two were yelling at one another. It reached such an intensity that the two had to be restrained and persuaded to calm down. Munson finally went back to his seat, hurt that Martin had taken out his anger on him.

When the plane landed in Chicago, Martin decided not to ride the team bus with the players. Instead, he took a cab to the hotel. Later, in the lobby, Yankee coaches Elston Howard, Yogi Berra, and Gene Michael were still talking with Munson, trying to get him to calm down and forget the entire incident.

The next day Martin apologized to Munson.

"What happened on the plane was completely a misunderstanding," explained Martin. "Thurman was right and I was wrong, and I'm going to tell him so. I have the greatest respect for Munson. I was hot and he wasn't. If anybody was at fault, I was.

"Thurman always teases me, and I had just come back to my seat from talking to somebody, and I wasn't in a very good mood. Thurman always gives me 100 percent. He's one of the best I ever had."

What upset Martin further was the fact that he wasn't getting solid support from his players over the Rivers incident. He had indicated to Munson that he was going to bench Rivers. Munson saw Martin's anger and tried to tell him just to relax and go out and have a good time. It was not what Martin wanted to hear at that moment.

Martin also talked with Lou Piniella. And he also had some words for Ken Holtzman, Rivers' closest friend on the team. In fact, Martin decided to give Holtzman a rare start that night against the White Sox. Perhaps he intended to showcase the little-used left-hander who expressed a desire to be traded because of his infrequent appearances. In any event, Martin, no matter how upsetting, was making his point that he wasn't happy with the way Rivers was playing. He felt the reason was that Holtzman was giving him bad advice.

"We're disgusted with the way Mickey is not hustling," admitted Piniella. "I know I am and others are, too. But Billy didn't help the situation the way he handled it. All he did was tick off Thurman and get on my back, too. I was mad at Mickey. I told him after the game, 'What the hell is going on here?'

"When we got to the plane, I was asked to play cards by Mickey and Holtzman. I've been playing cards with Mickey for three years now. Just because I'm mad at Mickey for lack of effort on the field doesn't mean I'm going to stop playing cards with him.

"Yet, Billy got teed off at me on the plane because I was playing cards with Mickey. To

Billy, that means that I'm not showing loyalty. That's bull. He would like for us to form a vigilante committee and deal with Rivers. But getting Mickey to cut out the garbage is the manager's job, not our job. Billy has to deal with it; and the way he botched it up, all he did was alienate others. He took one problem and stretched it into several. He's the boss and I respect that, but he has to be the boss."

Martin made up his mind. He did so alone. He decided that he would bench Rivers for his lackadaisical play. He wanted it understood that he wouldn't excuse anybody, no matter who it was, for not displaying hustle on the field.

"I'm sitting Rivers down in Chicago and in Cleveland and in Toronto and longer than that," emphasized Martin. "Paul Blair will be in centerfield. I want a guy out there who tries. Rivers says his leg hurts. Well, he can sit on the bench until he comes to me and tells me that he's ready to play. And I'm going to get rid of Holtzman within a week. He's gone. You can bet on it."

Martin's emphatic decision to bench Rivers had the full support of Rosen. Steinbrenner, who was away in Florida at the time, was informed by Rosen in New York of what had taken place.

"That's Billy's prerogative to bench Rivers," affirmed Rosen. "He's the manager on the field. That's his province. I'm 100 percent behind Billy. I know how much he wants to win; and he feels that if Rivers had played the game the way he can and should, the team would have won all three games in Kansas City.

"I also know that when October comes, Mickey will be hitting .325, and people will be saying that he's the best centerfielder in the American League. Billy knows it, too. But how do you get him to play 150 games?"

Apparently, by talking to him. Rivers also is a sensitive individual. First Howard and then coach Dick Howser told Rivers that Martin wanted to see him the next day in his hotel room at four o'clock. Yet, Rivers was adamant. He told both Howard and Howser that

(Above and opposite) Thurman Munson

he wouldn't be there unless Martin himself came to him and personally asked to see him.

"Why come to Lou and Thurman?" Rivers wanted to know. "Why get in a hassle with them? If you got a hassle with me, come talk to me. I'm like everybody else. I have feelings, too. He talks to others. Why can't he talk to me? If I don't play tonight, I don't know when I'm going to feel like playing. If I sit too long, I'm going to want to go somewhere else.

"I don't see why he carries on and carries on and carries on. I think you should talk to a man and get it over with. I told him I messed up. That's all I could tell him. I don't want to

look bad. Nobody wants to look bad, and nobody wants to be embarrassed.

"I think the whole thing was bad. You can't get the respect of people shouting like that. We can overlook it because anything can come out when a man is drinking. I don't hold that against anybody. He never asked me about my leg. I told him the leg was bad, but if he put me in the lineup, I'd go out and do my best. He talked rough to me, but I don't mind. I overlooked it because I want to go out and play and look good for the team."

But the team wasn't looking so good. Despite the many injuries, they had somehow managed to stay close to the Red Sox, who

had gotten off to a fast start. When May ended, the Yankees had improved their record to 29–17 and were only three games behind Boston.

When the Yankees faced the Red Sox for the first time later in June, they had fallen to seven games behind. Of even more concern, they had slipped to third place. Yet, the three-game series in Boston had provided them with an opportunity to pick up some valuable ground even though they still were plagued with injuries. Anyway, a Yankee-Red Sox series has a way of reviving a team that isn't doing so well.

Yet, Martin was a bit testy the day before the series opened. While his team was strug-

(Right) Red Sox action

(Below) Martin, Gullett, and Hunter

gling a bit, the Red Sox appeared as if they were on the verge of making the race a runaway. Their pitching was holding up, and their hitting looked even more awesome than during the previous season. Martin was looking to win two of the three games to shake the cobwebs from his squad.

"No one here is concerned at all," snapped Martin. "I don't care what my players say. I don't care what my coaches say. I don't care what the front office says. I speak for this team. And I don't care if we're ten games behind Boston, we are not concerned. We are still the world champions. Boston has to beat us.

"We're in this race. A seven-game difference means nothing. Nothing at all. Every game against Boston counts two, and there are a lot of games to go. A month from now we could be ahead by seven."

The players were aware that the three-game series with the Red Sox was important, if not crucial. They certainly didn't want to lose any more ground to Boston. Even though they were the champions, they were the ones who had to catch the Red Sox.

"I don't want to see the Red Sox getting too much confidence," remarked Jackson. "I don't want them thinking they're a much better ball club. They have enough momentum already. When we get together with the Red Sox, it's good old-fashioned hardball; and I love it. It's going to be like a little World Series.

"We're two powerful, gritty, fighting teams, clubs with great character. Mike Torrez has character. George Scott has character. Carl Yastrzemski has character. Players like Carlton Fisk, Jim Rice, and Fred Lynn are developing great competitive character.

"And we've got it here. Munson, Martin, Lyle, Nettles. I know I'm leaving names out. We're a fighting ball club, too. You've got to kick the hell out of us before we'll concede you're better. That's what fascinates me about Boston and New York. I think you've got the two best teams in baseball fighting each other in the same division, and they're both relentless in their character when it comes to playing hard, winning baseball. They just will not quit.

"Boston's got an axe to grind. They won 97 games last year, and it wasn't enough. They played great, and yet they lost the pennant. Wait. That's not right. They didn't lose. They were beaten, and there's a big difference there. So now they know they've got to play just a little bit harder. That gave them a little bit more grit. That's a plus for them.

"They have a better offensive ball club than we do. They're more devastating, especially in their own park. And Rice is the most destructive hitter I've ever seen. We've played poorly; Boston's played well. Very well. But there's only seven games between us with more than 100 games to go.

"That's not much, is it? They aren't going to run away from us. There's too much resiliency in this club. We're going to get our act together real soon. The hitting will come; you can bet on that. We've got some men here who can break games wide open. Pitching? Our starters will be okay. And Boston's got a good bullpen, but they don't have Lyle and Gossage.

"You read so much about the big money that's been paid to this team. That money was paid for a reason. We're winners. You see, winning, I mean winning big, winning championships, takes more than just physical talent. A lot of players have physical talent, but they're not winners. The Yankees are winners. So are the Red Sox. And we're going to have a fight to the finish."

Neither the Yanks nor the Red Sox wanted the other team to sweep. That would be dangerous. Last June the Red Sox swept the Yankees, outscoring them 30–9 and hitting 16 home runs in the process. Although the Yanks did manage to recover and go on to win the pennant, it nevertheless made them battle. And this year, Boston was a stronger team while the Yankees were not playing up to their championship level of a year ago.

"It will be a very important series to us psychologically," pointed out Cedric Tallis, the Yanks' general manager. "We must leave Boston with our dignity. Our problem is ob-

Willie Randolph

vious. Some of our players who performed very well last year have not maintained those standards this season. I'll tell you what bothers me about that. When you win a championship, there's a natural tendency for players to feel they can just throw their gloves onto the field and go right on winning the following year. It's a feeling they may not even be aware of. What happens is that they don't give that degree of extra effort. Consequently, they start losing.

"It's like playing ping pong. You'll be beating the hell out of somebody, and you'll start feeling sorry for him, so you let up a bit. Then you try to reach back and take charge again, and you find you can't always do it. That's what concerns me most of all. It's still early in the season, and it's entirely possible that our players will regain the momentum they had last season; but there's always the chance they'll reach back and find out they have nothing to grab. To be very cold-blooded about it, I think we're faced with one helluva battle to repeat as champions."

Chris Chambliss

One player who shared Tallis' concern was first baseman Chris Chambliss, who had managed to escape the injury list and play every game.

"I think there's a lot to be concerned about," said Chambliss. "We've got our hands full. Seven games is a lot to make up. You can say Boston is strong because of Fenway Park, but that's not really fair because the Red Sox are winning on the road, too. We're not, and that's what upsets me. We didn't get into this position by losing to

Boston. We're here because we've been losing to the teams we're supposed to beat."

That was Martin's feeling, too. It was the main reason that he seemed a bit uptight, that all he could think about was winning, perhaps even sweeping the Red Sox. That could turn it around for him and his club.

"Billy's a very demanding manager," said Piniella. "He gets perturbed when things aren't going right for us. Here we are, seven games behind Boston. We never thought that could happen. This is not a good situation to

Reggie Jackson and Billy Martin

Ed Figueroa

Graig Nettles

Reggie Jackson

Bucky Dent

Thurman Munson

Ron Guidry

be in. If it goes on much longer, Boston's going to be awfully tough to catch. There's no sense in kidding ourselves about that.

"We can beat Boston. We really can, but we can't beat them by saying so. We've got to do it on the field. I don't think you'll find a man in this clubhouse who doesn't believe we'll do it. The time has come. We've had our butts kicked long enough. The Red Sox are playing as well as they possibly can. Just excellent baseball. If they can continue doing that, then all I can say is, more power to them. But if they start to falter a bit, and I've never seen a club that didn't have some dry spells, then we're going to give them something to think about.

"We're going to turn it around. There's no way we're going to die while Boston runs away with it. This is a club that's been able to bounce back from adversity before. Whenever we've had our backs to the wall, we've been able to fight back and play better baseball. Well, that's where we're at right now. It's time to start playing good baseball. The next 15 or 20 games are going to be very important to us."

The Yankees' hopes of returning to the championship form expected of them in Boston were dimmed. The Red Sox took the series, 2–1, and increased their lead over the beleaguered champions to eight games. By the time the All-Star game arrived, the Yanks were in third place, 11½ games out, after dropping three straight games in Milwaukee. They were heading downward with a 46–38 record.

Piniella's remark about the next 20 games was prophetic. Twenty-two games later, the Yanks' record had dipped to 47–41. Martin was now under tremendous strain and pressure. His champions had fallen 13 games behind the surging Red Sox. Most experts were beginning to write off the Yankees. It pained Martin to hear the stories circulating that his team was dead.

Martin had begun to look tired and haggard. Martin's physical ailment was described as a stubborn virus that he had been unable to overcome all season. Steinbrenner, sensing that Martin might crack under pressure, suggested to his manager that it might be better if he resigned for health reasons. The ailment that was described as a virus turned out to be a spot on Martin's liver. Martin, a

Reggie Jackson, violating Billy Martin's order to hit away, pops up a strike in a bunt attempt during the tenth inning of a loss to Kansas City. The Yankees suspended Jackson after the game. (World Wide Photos)

fighter all his life, rejected Steinbrenner's offer.

"I'm not a quitter," snapped Martin. "I want to try to win this thing. I owe it to the Yankee fans."

The once bubbly Martin became more withdrawn. He didn't joke or laugh much anymore. It was hard for him. Instead, he tried to relax after a game by taking a couple of drinks, which certainly didn't help his liver condition. Still, he refused to enter a hospital for treatment. He felt that if he did, he would be removed as manager of the Yankees, with the shuddering thought that he might never be able to return because of health reasons. He didn't want any part of that. No fighter does.

The night the Yankees fell 14 games behind, Martin went into a post-game rage. After losing the first two games to the Royals in Yankee Stadium, the Yanks were struggling to try to salvage the third and final game. The teams battled to a 5–5 tie and went to the tenth inning. Munson opened the extra inning with a single. Jackson was up next, and on the first pitch he was given a bunt sign. The pitch from reliever Al Hrabosky was a ball.

The bunt sign was then removed. However, on the next pitch, Jackson tried to bunt and fouled the ball off. Third base coach Dick Howser called time and trotted over to Jackson.

"Billy wants you to hit away," instructed Howser.

"I'm gonna bunt," answered Jackson.

"He wants you to swing the bat," explained Howser.

"I'm gonna bunt," repeated Jackson.

Hrabosky delivered the pitch, and again Jackson tried to bunt. Again he fouled off the pitch. Martin couldn't believe what was happening. Jackson stepped back into the batter's box and, instead of swinging away, attempted to bunt for the third straight time. He fouled the ball up in the air behind home plate, and catcher Darrell Porter caught the ball for the out.

The Royals completed the three-game sweep of the Yankees by scoring four runs in the eleventh inning for a 9–7 victory. As soon as the game was over, Martin closed the door of his office. When he opened the door to the press, Martin had an announcement to make. He did all he could do to avoid exploding as he read a hastily prepared, handwritten statement.

"Reggie Jackson is suspended without pay effective this moment for deliberately disregarding the manager's instructions during his time at bat in the tenth inning," began Martin. "The bunt was on, on the first pitch. It was then taken off via verbal instructions by the third base coach. The manager's orders were just disregarded. He bunted in direct defiance of a verbal order to hit."

Martin put down the statement. Then with Tallis, who met with Martin and Howser behind locked doors, standing next to him, Martin continued in an emotional voice.

"There's not gonna be anybody who's gonna defy the manager or management in any way," declared Martin. "Nobody's bigger than this team. I sensed by Jackson's attitude when he came to the ball park today that he was very upset about something. His attitude up until today has been tremendous. If he comes back, he does exactly what I say, period. I'm not getting paid $3 million. I don't disobey my boss's orders. He tells me to do something and I do it."

Martin didn't say a word to Jackson. He was too upset to talk to him. Jackson was told of his suspension by reporters.

"I'd just like to know how long I'm going to be suspended so I can go to California and relax for a few days," exclaimed Jackson. "The guy's been doing this to me for a year-and-a-half now. Just yesterday he called me over and asked me to sit next to him in the dugout and said, 'You're a nice guy. You're a fine guy. I just wanted to tell you that.'

"I can't win. No matter what I do I come off as the big, greedy moneymaker against a poor, little street fighter."

When Jackson returned to the dugout after his bunting folly, first base coach Gene Michael told him on instructions from Martin

(Above) Roy White

(Right) Ed Figueroa

that Roy White was the DH and that he could shave and go home if he wanted to. But Jackson remained on the bench.

"I stayed and watched the ball game and pulled for the guys," said Jackson. "I figured that I'd advance Munson the best way I could. If I get a man in scoring position with Lou Piniella coming up behind me, I figured we'd have a pretty good chance to win the ball game. I think if I had been successful, it would have wound up different. If it would have been someone else, all this wouldn't be going on."

But it did. Earlier that day, Jackson met privately with Steinbrenner for more than an hour. He apparently was upset about the fact that he was made a designated hitter the week before with Munson taking his position in rightfield. It was a move that Steinbrenner approved, and Jackson expressed his displeasure at being the DH and not playing the field. Now he was suspended for five days, which cost him some $12,000 in pay.

Strangely, Jackson's suspension didn't hurt the Yankees. Quite to the contrary. Although reeling 14 games behind Boston, the Yanks got shutout pitching from Ed Figueroa and Ron Guidry and swept the Twins in Minnesota. Then they moved on to Chicago and took all three games from the White Sox. The Yanks' sharp surge cut Boston's margin to 10 games. The team appeared loose. In fact, instead of causing any friction, Jackson's suspension seemed to make the team more harmonious.

"If the ownership would back me like that on everything, my job would be easy," philosophized Martin.

It was obvious Martin was operating with the full support of management. Like Martin, perhaps even more so, Steinbrenner will not tolerate insubordination. His German ancestry and military school background dictated that. Al Rosen emphasized the front office's position.

"The manager runs the club on the field," said Rosen. "He has the full authority to do this and the full backing of the front office on this matter. No player or players are bigger than the team. That's the way I played and that's the way I run this team."

The players also seemed to support Martin. They demonstrated that by going on a modest, four-game winning streak before Jackson rejoined the team on the final day of the Chicago series. In Jackson's absence, Martin calmed down somewhat, even making plans to talk to his defiant star.

"I'm going to have my coaches there and maybe even a tape recorder so there's no misunderstanding of what I have to tell him," said Martin. "I wanted to make sure he understands completely the following four points: Number one, I don't dislike him; number two, he can't play rightfield; number three, he can hit; and number four, if he ever does something like this again, I'll fine him and suspend him.

"I'm an easy guy to play for. All I ever ask of a player is to hustle and obey orders. They'll never have any trouble with me if they do that.

"I don't want any apologies or anything like that. I just want him to go to his locker, get dressed, and go out and do his job. He'll be in the lineup for Sunday's game."

Jackson did return as expected for Sunday's game against the White Sox. He didn't ask to see Martin. He kept a low profile as if nothing had happened, but he did manage to talk to a group of reporters in front of his locker before the game. It had all the atmosphere of a conquering hero returning to battle. Martin was alone in his office, and the excitement that Jackson created made him do a slow burn. Instead of telling stories and joking around as he had earlier in the week, Martin seemed a bit tense. It was Jackson who was loose and talkative to the press.

"It was difficult, but I can't say I had any visions of not reporting," began Jackson. "It's uncomfortable being me. It's uncomfortable being recognized constantly. It's uncomfortable being considered something I'm not, an idol or a monster, something hated or loved.

"I've tried to talk to God. I've talked to religious people, but I've got to make the decision myself. I'm the guy who is involved, and nobody can really make a decision for me."

Naturally, the subject of his bunting came

Roy White

up. Jackson didn't duck the question. Surprisingly, he still maintained that what he did was right.

"I hadn't been playing consistently, so I felt bunting to advance the runner at first base was my best shot. I'd probably do the same thing because I didn't realize what the consequences would be. I didn't regard it as an act of defiance. If I had known the consequences would have this magnitude, I would rather have swung and struck out and avoided the hassle.

"I don't know if I'm going to apologize. For the way they interpreted the offense, an apology is in order. But the way I interpreted it, I don't think what I did was so wrong. I'm sorry I caused the guys on the club grief and uncomfort. I don't want to cause them any grief. I'd like to see them win the next 70 games. It would take the pressure off me."

It was Martin under pressure now. Sitting in his office making out his lineup, he didn't pencil Jackson's name in. He had an explanation, saying he hadn't seen Jackson to learn if he had done any hitting. Then he emphasized his point.

"You kind of think he'd be out here earlier and want to hit," snapped Martin. "But apparently he didn't want to."

So Jackson sat in the dugout and watched his teammates win their fifth straight game without him. He saw Roy White, who took his place as the designated hitter, collect three hits, steal a base, and score a run. And he saw the Yankees break a tight 1–1 game in the ninth inning by scoring two runs for the victory, and consequently stay within 10 games of the Red Sox. The Yankees seemed to be coming alive.

Martin was very much so after the game. He had his chance with newsmen at O'Hare Airport some two hours later as the Yanks were preparing to fly to Kansas City. It was obvious that the remarks that Jackson made before the game had gotten back to him. He bristled. He didn't like what Jackson had said. He practically told him to shut up.

"We're winning without Jackson," fumed Martin. "We don't need him coming in and making all these comments. If he doesn't shut his mouth, he won't play and I don't care what Steinbrenner says. He can replace me right now if he doesn't like it.

"We have a smooth-running ship here, and I don't want him and his mouth coming along and breaking it up. If he wants to play ball, just shut up and play. I don't want to hear any more from him.

"It's like a guy getting out of jail and saying 'I'm innocent' after he killed somebody. He and every one of the other players knew he defied me. Why else did he take his glasses off when he came back to the bench? He expected to get popped but good. It was the most control it's ever taken in my life not to hit him."

The plane that would fly the Yanks to Kansas City wouldn't depart for another hour. So Martin, in an attempt to relax, went to the airport bar. There were a couple of New York reporters there, and Martin drank and talked with them. He was still disturbed by the remarks that Jackson had made. Then Martin and the writers started for the departure gate.

"They deserve each other," remarked Martin. "One is a born liar (Jackson), and the other is convicted (Steinbrenner)."

The writers couldn't believe what they heard. Martin's remarks were extremely damaging, strong enough to have him reprimanded or fired. Later that night the two writers phoned Steinbrenner at his home in Florida and informed him of what Martin had said. Steinbrenner couldn't believe it, either. The rest of the night Steinbrenner was on the phone talking to Martin, Tallis, and reporters. It was clear that Martin was doomed.

The next morning Steinbrenner sent Rosen and the club's public relations director, Mickey Morabito, to Kansas City. The owner wanted to have his aides ease Martin out of his job gracefully. He didn't want to fire Martin or embarrass him in any way. Steinbrenner was well aware of Martin's popularity with the New York fans.

After hours of telephone conversations and meetings, it was arranged for Martin to resign. Morabito called a hastily arranged press conference. It was scheduled, of all places, in front of an antique shop on the mezzanine of the Crown Center Hotel. Martin, appearing haggard, arrived on time with a friend, Bob Brown. Before he read from a handwritten statement on hotel stationery, Martin prefaced his remarks:

"I want to tell you right now that there will be no questions, not now, not afterwards, or ever, because Yankees don't throw rocks."

Then he looked down at his sheet of paper that was written on both sides and began:

"I don't want to hurt this team's chances for the pennant with all this undue publicity. The team has a shot at the pennant, and I hope they win it. I owe it to my health and my mental well-being to resign. At this time I am also sorry about these things that were written about George Steinbrenner. He doesn't deserve them . . . nor did I say them. George and I have had our differences, and in most cases we've been able to resolve them."

The emotion was too much. Martin began to cry. His voice cracked as he attempted to finish saying what he had written.

"I would like to thank the Yankee management, the press, the news media, my coaches, my players, and most of all . . . the fans."

Martin was distraught. He couldn't continue. He was crying to the point of shaking. He was led away by Rosen and Brown down a corridor and out a service entrance, crying all the way.

Morabito finished the last line of Martin's statement that Billy had written but couldn't say:

"And most of all, the fans for their undying support."

Phil Rizzuto, the Yankees' broadcaster, witnessed Martin's resignation with a great deal of emotion himself. A former teammate, Rizzuto is one of Martin's closest friends.

"I thought the bottom of the world had dropped out watching him make that statement and break down," remarked Rizzuto. "I was really afraid he was going to have a heart attack. The Yankees were his whole life. He always talked about finished his career with New York and managing the Yankees. It probably was the worst news I heard in baseball, except in 1956 when they told me I was released."

Despite the fact that he resigned, the Yanks were going to honor Martin's contract, which had a year remaining. That meant that Martin would receive the balance of his $80,000 salary for 1978 and $90,000 for 1979. Steinbrenner insisted on paying it.

"We have never worked better together than we have the last two or three weeks," said Steinbrenner about Martin. "On learning of the Chicago thing, I was shocked. You could have knocked me over.

"The events that have transpired in the last hours have little significance when compared to a man's concern for his own well-being. These things, along with his family, are far more important than the game of baseball.

"I am grateful to Billy for his contributions as manager of the Yankees. He brought us a championship. His apologies over the recent incident are accepted with no further comment necessary. I think Billy knows of our concern for the well-being of his family and himself. We wish him good luck."

Down deep, Steinbrenner likes Martin. He likes his fiery spirit, his relentless drive to win, his colorful personality. But after the flagrant remarks that Martin had made, Billy had to go. Even Rosen made that clear when he arrived in Kansas City.

"I came here because as president of the Yankees I could not allow any statement made by Billy Martin about George Steinbrenner to go unchallenged," pointed out Rosen.

And while it was Rosen's objective to insure an orderly resignation, he also was saddled with the responsibility of securing a new manager in a short period of time. He did so by convincing his one-time Cleveland teammate, Bob Lemon, to take over. Two days later, Lemon joined the Yankees in Kansas City from his home in California.

Ironically, Lemon had been dismissed as manager of the White Sox only a month earlier. Not only did Jackson's return put pressure on Martin, but while he was in Chicago Martin suffered another blow. He learned from White Sox owner Bill Veeck about a possible swap of managers. Lee MacPhail, the president of the American League, had suggested to Veeck in June that perhaps trading Lemon for Martin might be a solution for both clubs. The Sox were losing, and Martin was under a strain in New York; a change may be beneficial.

Just the thought of it tore Martin up inside. All he ever wanted was to manage the Yankees, and now he learned that he was suggested in a trade. How serious the thought was didn't matter. What did matter was that Martin's Yankee world was shaken. The revelation only served to make him feel more insecure. Naturally, it affected his mood. Possibly he felt betrayed. He had been through enough already.

"Billy was taking care of all our problems, and maybe it just wore him out," remarked Mickey Rivers.

Lemon, a quiet but firm disciplinarian, brought an air of calm to the ball club. He had an easygoing way about him, but underneath he was tough. He, too, was a firm believer in rules. He wouldn't tolerate anyone who broke them, no matter who they were. It would be a mistake for any player to try to take advantage of his good nature.

Still, Lemon realized that he was replacing a volatile yet popular Martin. When Martin resigned, he tugged at the hearts of the New York fans. Yankee Stadium's switchboard was deluged with calls. So were the city's newspaper boards. When the Yankees returned to the Stadium for the first time under Lemon on July 26, there were a number of banners supporting Martin. Souvenir vendors were hawking Billy Martin buttons, originally priced at $1.50, for $2, calling them collectors' items. Martin might have left quietly, but the fans were vociferous in their support of him.

On Old Timer's Day three days later, the Yanks had crept to within eight games of the Red Sox. In 10 games they had made up six lengths. It certainly provided the Yankees with much more hope. And what better time could the Yankees gain added momentum than Old Timer's Day, with such legendary greats as Joe DiMaggio, Mickey Mantle, Roger Maris, Yogi Berra, and Whitey Ford on hand?

The introduction of past Yankee stars drew applause from the crowd. Public address announcer Bob Sheppard arrived at Lemon's introduction. There was something extra to announce. As he talked, the big electric scoreboard flashed the message that Lemon would become the general manager in 1980.

Something was up. The crowd buzzed, then Sheppard continued.

"Managing the Yankees in the 1980 season," he began, "and hopefully for many seasons after that, will be Number One . . . Billy Martin!"

The big crowd stood and roared as Martin ran up the dugout steps and onto the field. Billy Martin was coming back indeed. They began to applaud with gusto. Martin shook hands with Lemon, embraced his friend Rizzuto, and stood in line next to Berra. He took off his hat to the crowd, his crowd. They stood cheering. They gave him a seven-minute ovation that was unprecedented in the history of the Yankees, even bigger than that given to Babe Ruth or Lou Gehrig. Just five days after he had reached the pits, Martin climbed the heights.

Martin's appearance took everyone by surprise, the current players as well as the old timers. He was sequestered in a room, protected by special security guards, as he put on his Yankee uniform. No one saw him until he made his appearance on the field.

"All of a sudden Billy Martin ran past me up the steps onto the field as they were announcing that he'd be back as manager in 1980," exclaimed DiMaggio. "I was stunned. I figured he'd make an appearance for the Old Timer's Day, but nothing like this. Unbelievable."

Even Mantle, his closest friend with an undying loyalty to Martin, was amazed.

"Two years ago on a golf course, somebody told me that Billy got fired by the Yankees and asked how I'd feel about it," said Mantle. "You were always hearing that he was getting fired. I said that if I thought he got ripped off, I'd probably never go back to New York again. He's closer to me than my brothers.

"But I talked to Billy this week after he quit, and I was certain that he'd had a choice this time. He'd made up his mind to quit even before Al Rosen got on the plane and flew to Kansas City to confront him. Anyway, this time I never had to make that decision not to come back."

Rizzuto still couldn't believe what had taken place, but at least he was happy.

"Unbelievable," exclaimed Rizzuto. "Barnum and Bailey. Like the guy who jumped off the Brooklyn Bridge. But it's unbelievable. I've read the whole Frank Merriwell series of baseball tales, and the closest he came to anything like this was when he discovered how to pitch the double-shoot. Unbelievable.

"I talked to Billy on Tuesday and Wednesday, the two days after he quit. And whenever we'd talk about the Yankees, he'd start crying. I'll tell you, somebody's got a touch of genius here."

It was Steinbrenner. He put the entire

(This page and opposite) Billy
Martin's return

(Left) Al Rosen and George Steinbrenner at press conference on subject of Martin's rehiring

(Below) Martin's return

melodramatic proceedings together from his home in Tampa. He didn't even fly into New York until Friday evening. All week long he had talked to Rosen, Martin, and Martin's agent Doug Newton, and worked out the details of not only rehiring Martin but also of his appearance on Old Timer's Day. Ironically, it was exactly three years earlier on the same occasion that Steinbrenner had first hired Martin to manage the Yankees.

Afterward, at a special press conference,

Steinbrenner's statements on the rehiring of Martin were released in a prepared statement. It read:

"There was no fan reaction or lack of fan reaction that precipitated this decision, nor was there anything that was read or printed or not printed that precipitated it. Right after the All-Star break, Al and I first talked about Billy's situation and the health that Billy alluded to on the West Coast. Then, as early as Monday morning (in the wee hours), Doug

New York Yankees

Newton, who I had been in contact with all week and who is Billy's manager, were in contact by phone.

"What transpired in the ensuing week was almost constant conversations between Al Rosen and myself and Doug Newton so that this is not something that was arrived at on the spur of the moment. It's something that we have given a great deal of consideration to.

"Now, I am probably going to be undoubt-edly ripped a little for being soft maybe or being stupid, but let me tell you this: There are times in life when you should be tough and times when you have to be rigid, and there are times when you have to be under-standing and have compassion. And I am not trying to sound corny, I am trying to tell you exactly what happened.

"Al and I discussed this at length, and I told him my feelings. I told him that in my gut, as much had gone on both ways, that I didn't feel what had happened was right. Well I've always thought better with my gut than my heart and if being compassionate toward a man who has the courage to admit he has a concern for his health and emotional well-being, and who came to me after his resignation when he had nothing really to gain, and said he was sorry for what he had said, and admitted that he had committed an indiscretion in denying it—if caring about wanting to work with and help that man is a sign of softness—then I'd helluva lot rather be called soft and stupid than a rock and brilliant.

"Al and I spent many hours discussing it. You know, what took place in Chicago, I can't hide. I was convicted of an election violation. That's part of life, that's what you live with, and I live with the plaques and few honors that I managed to get the same way I live with that; and it's going to come up again and again, and I should live with it, and that had no real part, and should have no real part unless I am a pretty selfish individual, in what happened.

"Billy Martin came to me after he had resigned. What he said to me showed me that he was a man who realized that maybe he had made a small mistake, and it was small in the total picture. We had many talks, I shouldn't say many, I should say two, and many phone conversations. I firmly believe that the biggest challenge in this thing doesn't lie with me, with the Yankees. The biggest challenge of all lies with Billy. He referred to his health problem, it's a problem that he has been told will not be serious if he looks after it. He spoke of the emotional situation in the way that he was so uptight, and under so much pressure, and I believe the man, and I believe what he has told me.

"He's going to get the rest he needs, and he's going to do exactly what his doctor has told us he must do. I have that commitment from him in spades. I believe in him and Al does also and we just feel that we are with Billy in this thing. The burden of the proof and the burden of the challenge lies with Billy. Billy is going to attack both challenges and we are going to be with him on it. You

might say Billy and I have been down this road before—well never like this, let me assure you. It'll work if Billy really wants it bad enough, and I believe he does.

"He will spend the next year-and-a-half working with us, evaluating our talent and working with Al and Bob Lemon. Then in 1980, hopefully, we'll get his clearance to join us and be with us (and that his health will be where he wants it), so he'll be ready to tackle the challenge of assuming again the managerial duties of the New York Yankees and be with us for many years. Nothing would make either Al or I happier than to have that work out that way, and so that all the things that have happened in the past are meaningless."

Martin also spoke at the conference, in which there were no questions allowed. He was brief but was happy and relieved.

"I would like to say that, as you know, George and I in the past have had our indifferences, but we always found a way sometimes to solve them," began Martin. "I am very proud at this moment at the wonderful thing that he has done for me. This is the home where I want to be, more than anything else. This is the only managing job I've ever wanted.

"When I quit the other day, I called George and told him how I apologized for what was said. I did say it, I don't know why I said it—I was angered at the time; I had no reason to say it, and I feel very bad about it, and I am not afraid to admit as much. I know that when I do come back, as the manager of the Yankees, that our relationship will be tremendous. Now I have a second chance, thanks to George. I know what my problems are and I'm gonna lick them. The challenge is there for me. I'm gonna do whatever I can for George—he deserves it.

"I am going to work twice as hard at it, in other fields, fields that I have never done before. I am a free spirit, and I am going to try to do other things that George wants me to do, and at the same time, he says that he is going to try and be a little more free-spirited too. But I think our association is going to be fabulous, and I thank Bob Lemon very much for his understanding of all this, because as you know, he has always been a class guy in my eyes, and I am sure he is in yours, and also Al Rosen's."

One who wasn't taken with Martin's projected return was Jackson. In fact, he felt somewhat threatened by the turn of events.

"I just don't think I'll be here when Martin comes back," admitted Jackson. "I hear some of the people in the front office think it's a good thing to have to be dealt. And I don't mean dealt a pat hand out of Vegas. I feel it's 50-50 I won't finish the season here. It takes the blame off them and puts it on me."

Almost lost in the excitement of Old Timer's Day was the fact that the present Yankees had 61 games left to overtake Boston. By August 11 they had crept up to within 6½ games of first place. However, they lost their next two games to the Baltimore Orioles; and by August 13 they fell nine games behind.

Still, the interest in Martin and Jackson continued. A week after he was hired back, Martin held an informal press conference over lunch at a restaurant not too far from Yankee Stadium. Martin was tanned and relaxed and willing to talk freely.

"I still don't have any malice or dislike in my heart for Reggie Jackson," began Martin. "I've done everything I can to help the young man, and now he has to help himself. Yet, he was the basis for my resignation, that and a slip of the tongue, saying something I didn't want to say and didn't think would be printed. I didn't mean it about George, and I probably said it in jest; but I did mean it

Reggie Jackson

Bucky Dent and Fred Stanley

about the other guy. There's no question about it. Any man who makes a mistake and won't admit it is a weak man.

"I was mad at Jackson. The club was winning and relaxed, and he comes back and won't admit he made a mistake. He said he bunted because he was thinking of the next hitter. Did it ever occur to him they might walk Piniella? That's what they pay managers for, to think about the next batter.

"I thought after Reggie came back he would say that he made a mistake. Like a man. But when I read that he didn't think he had made a mistake at all, that set me off. He'd been away five days when he came back; but he didn't take batting practice, and

I didn't know even if he had swung a bat in five days.

"He was fined by the manager. It was okayed by the owner, and he denied it. Between Reggie coming back and sitting around saying he didn't think he did anything wrong, well, I thought the situation wasn't a good working condition as far as I was concerned.

"I couldn't sleep that night at all. I got up early and paced the floor and made up my mind to resign. I called Steinbrenner later in the day to apologize. I just wanted him to know that it was a terrible thing to say, but I meant what I said about the other guy.

"Wherever he's played he's always had

problems with the manager. If Reggie is here in 1980, he can expect to be treated like one of 25 players with the same privileges as anyone else. And if he abuses them, he'll get his hand spanked again. No player can dictate policy to the manager. When he does, you don't need a manager.

"There's nothing wrong with my health. I have no problem with my liver. I've just got to eat more often than when I was managing.

By the end of August the Yankees had won seven straight games and cut Boston's lead to 6½ games.

In September the Yanks won five of the first seven games they played. The Red Sox experienced difficulty winning. They dropped seven out of nine games, and suddenly the Yankees were only four games behind. The Red Sox had to look over their shoulders now. They couldn't avoid it. They

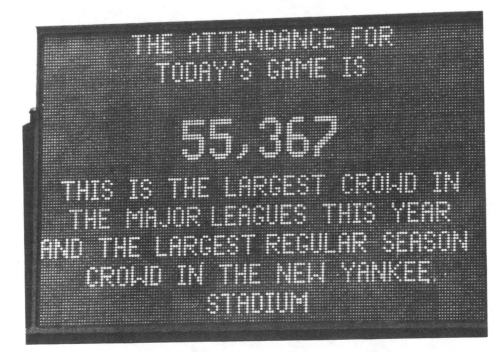

In fact, I'm taking pills to make me eat more. As for drinking, the doctor said I can have up to four mixed drinks a night. My health wasn't a consideration at all in my resignation. I miss managing already. I don't think I'll ever be away from it."

The Yankees still felt they weren't far away from first place. They held tough. Slowly, they started putting it all together. For the first time all season the Yanks were healthy again. Catfish Hunter came off the disabled list and began to win. Ed Figueroa shook off his arm miseries and began to win consistently. So did Jim Beattie. Rivers, Jackson, Nettles, and White began to hit consistently, and Bucky Dent began to play more often.

had to face the Yankees in a four-game series in Fenway Park beginning on September 7. Everyone knew how important the series was. Suddenly, there was a hot pennant race that no one expected.

The Red Sox were still in command. They had the four-game lead. They had beaten the Yankees in six of the eight games played up until then, but the Yankees were hot. Since July 19 they were 35–14, which is an amazing .714 pace. Boston had to be aware of that streak. It was much the same for them when they started off the season at such a fast pace. Now, from 14 games it was down to four.

"This is what it's all about," exclaimed Lemon. "It isn't exactly where I'd like to be.

Rich Gossage

I'd like to be here five games in front. But really, we couldn't ask for more, considering. We have to win two. We can't come out of here with less than a split."

The players were looking for more. They felt confident of winning more than two games.

"I'd say our chances are good," said Figueroa. "Everything rides on what we do now. We weren't playing well before we went to Boston the other times, and we didn't improve any. But now we are playing good baseball. We have good pitching; but what's

important is that we are hitting, too. And the hitting can help us there."

Gossage seemed excited by the four-game series. He had never played on a strong pennant contender before.

"The closest I've come to pitching an important game was with the White Sox in '72," disclosed Gossage. "But we weren't really that close. I haven't been in a situation like this probably since I was nine years old. I pitched a no-hitter in Colorado Springs. I feel I've missed something since. But as much as I'd like to pitch in games like these,

Catfish Hunter

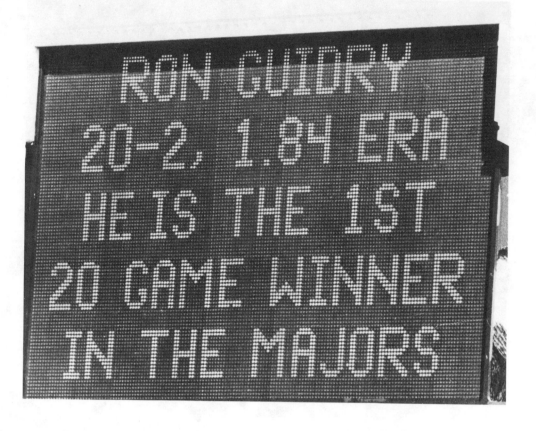

I'd just as soon not pitch if it means the starters are doing their job. I'll just sit back, rest, and enjoy the sweep.

"They got to hear us breathing. You bet they do. We're playing good ball right now, and I am not so sure the Red Sox are. When we were 14 games out, it didn't look very good. To tell you the truth, I never lost hope, but I can remember thinking how hard it would be. I remember sitting and talking with some of the guys saying, 'Wow, can you imagine if we pull this thing off? That would be something.'

"I've never seen a team like this. I can't believe the look in their eyes. It's like they know they are going to sweep."

Lemon had Hunter ready for the opening game. He had Beattie for game two, Guidry for game three, and Figueroa for game four. He was going with his top four starters. His starting rotation was set.

Before the game, Red Sox centerfielder Dwight Evans noticed that the wind was blowing in. He didn't like that.

"The wind's blowing in, and that's not good," remarked Evans. "When it blows in from left here, it works against us. It's a disadvantage for us. Really, it can be an asset for the Yankees."

The Yankees scored the very first time at bat. They kept pounding away at starter Mike Torrez, knocking him out in the second inning when they scored three more times. After four innings, they belted their way to a 12–0 lead. The Red Sox were shocked. By the time the game was over, they were utterly speechless. The Yankees sprayed 21 hits around Fenway Park for an easy 15–3 triumph.

The outcome was never in doubt. Willie Randolph had a big night by driving in five runs. Jackson, who wasn't expected to play because he had just been released from the hospital where he had spent a day in traction, contributed to the 21-hit assault with an RBI single. However, the Yankees felt some concern. Hunter had to leave with a 12–0 lead after three innings because of a pulled groin muscle. Munson was beaned on the forehead with a fastball thrown by Dick

Drago in the sixth inning. However, the gritty catcher said he would be able to play the next night.

"We haven't played this well since God knows when," said Piniella after the game. "It's only one win, but it probably means more to us than it does to them. But still, it's only one win. If we go on to win the next three, then we can look back and say, 'Yeah, that was a big win.' But right now, it's just a win. We showed we're a finesse team, and we beat a team that has hurt us with its power. That's important."

Lemon felt the opening-game win was also important. If the Yanks had lost, the pressure would have mounted.

"We had to win the first one here," replied Lemon. "It showed us something. We could say that the Red Sox are catchable and say we have a chance. This is the first time we've had a chance to do the damage to them ourselves, and we did it. Not with talk. We beat them with our bats and gloves and arms."

Evans also felt that the loss was significant. Especially the way the Red Sox were beaten.

"You don't like to be routed in any game," explained Evans. "But especially in a game like this. We haven't been playing that well lately, and a game like this could be demoralizing. I don't think it will be, but it could be."

It remained to be seen. The Yanks were only three games out as Beattie went against Jim Wright. They really didn't need Munson. Led by home runs by Jackson and Piniella, the Yanks bombed Boston pitching for 17 more hits on the way to a 13-2 rout. After a first inning double by Fred Lynn, Beattie retired 19 Red Sox in order in pitching a strong game. The easy win, nevertheless, provided the Yanks with another worry. Rivers pulled a hamstring muscle in beating out an infield hit and wasn't expected to play the following day.

Now the Yanks were only two games behind. What made them feel more confident was the fact that Guidry would be pitching against Boston's ace, Dennis Eckersley. Guidry was looking for his 21st victory while Eckersley was seeking to improve his 16-6 record. He, too, was confident.

"I regard pitching against Guidry as a challenge," exclaimed Eckersley. "I haven't had too many challenges this season."

It was one he should have avoided. Guidry was magnificent. He blanked Boston on two hits in achieving his first decision over the Red Sox, 7-0. The Yankees continued their hitting spree. They chased Eckersley in the fourth inning when they scored all their runs. Guidry ballooned his record to 21-2 and became the first left-hander to blank Boston in Fenway Park since Ken Holtzman did it when he pitched for the Oakland Athletics in 1974.

"I think you have to pitch inside to their right-handed hitters, challenging their power," explained Guidry. "I thought about it all Friday night. Our club is scoring a lot of runs. Then you have a Saturday afternoon game where two guys who have been doing a great job for their clubs are going against each other. You figure it could be a low-scoring game or one of them is going to be lit up. You just hope and pray that you're not the guy who gets lit up.

"I didn't let the ball park scare me. Besides, the wind was blowing in. So why not take a few chances? I threw one inside pitch to Jim Rice that he might have hit out if the wind wasn't blowing and if he had expected it. But they don't expect lefties to pitch the power hitters inside here. I didn't want to throw away from their power all game, either, because these guys can hit home runs to rightfield, too."

But they didn't. Boston was starting to feel the pressure. Only one game separated them from the surging Yankees.

"It's about time that somebody put pressure on these guys," exclaimed Dent. "They've had it their own way. The pressure right now is on them, not on us. If we come out tomorrow and score two runs in the first inning, they're dead."

Boston manager Don Zimmer hoped to keep his team alive by starting a rookie pitcher in the fourth and final game of the series. Zimmer was gambling that 21-year-old Bob Sprowl, who had pitched only one game in the majors, five days earlier, would stop the Yankees. Zimmer's choice of the green rook-

Willie Randolph

ie angered veteran right-hander Luis Tiant. The ageless Cuban told Zimmer that he wanted to pitch the final game even though he had only three days' rest.

"Nobody but me is pitching tomorrow," snapped Tiant to Zimmer. "I get the ball."

However, Zimmer refused to listen to Tiant. Instead, he announced that Sprowl would face Ed Figueroa.

"I'm glad he has that kind of confidence in me," remarked Sprowl. "After all, I've got only one game under my belt here. I throw mostly a fastball. I've also got a slider, and I've been working on a change. My goal is to keep us in the game. I wouldn't expect to pitch a shutout."

The Red Sox hope was that if Sprowl could keep the Yanks close, then their hitting, which hadn't surfaced in the first three games, would eventually overcome New York. They definitely needed to salvage the final game.

"I'm not down; the team's not down," revealed Yastrzemski. "There's no way we should be. I've seen this team bounce back, win nine of ten games. The big thing is that we're still in first place. We'll snap out of it. I've never seen a pennant come easy around here."

Sprowl couldn't keep the Yanks close. He couldn't do anything. He was chased in the first inning when the Yanks scored three

Brian Doyle

times on the way to a 7–4 victory and a sweep of the series. They were now tied with Boston for first place. The odds of sweeping the Red Sox in Boston were astronomical. Yet, the Yankees did it.

"We knew we needed two of these games," remarked Jackson. "We were hoping for three. Four? I don't think any of us thought about it. Who would have believed it?"

The Red Sox couldn't. In the four games they were completely overwhelmed. The Yankees outscored them, 42–9, and outhit them, 67–21. In a sense, it was a massacre. The Red Sox were humiliated in their own park.

"They shellacked us," moaned Zimmer. "That's all there is to it. I don't know what happened. For four days I looked at the scoreboard in the third or fourth inning, and we're trailing by five or six runs and they have 12 or 15 hits. I've been in baseball a long time, and I know anything can happen in this game. But I didn't think this could happen. I didn't think any team could sweep this Red Sox team in four games at home. Damn."

While the Red Sox clubhouse was sad and quiet, the Yankees were loose and happy. It was as if they had won the pennant. One thing was certain: they had taken a big step in that direction. The players felt that way.

"When a team has won a championship before, like we have, it knows what it has to do to win again," pointed out Piniella. "And now we're finally doing it. We play better when we're leading. I don't see any reason why we can't go on playing like we have for the past seven weeks. We can win. We can win this thing.

"The sweep here may have given us an edge. I don't know. Things in a race like this can change in a few days. We've just got to go out and play hard and see what happens. The season is 20 games long now."

Graig Nettles

What the Yankees had done now was win six straight games, and 16 of 18. Since Lemon took over, they had won 36 of 49 games, a phenomenal .735 pace. That's far more than a pennant pace. It's out of sight. Yet, Lemon didn't want to take credit for turning the Yanks around.

"The team had won five in a row when I got the club," replied Lemon. "When I took over, it was a week before I knew what was going on. It's been our pitching that has been outstanding. That brought us back. I haven't had much to do with it because this club is loaded with all kinds of talent.

"Does anybody but me find this hard to believe? This is a crazy game. I can't figure it out. We came into Fenway looking for a split and go out with a hatful. The first game, we won so big it made us looser for the other three games; no question about it. I don't know how it affected the Boston club.

"But I'm not kidding myself into thinking that this thing is over. We go right back at it next weekend in New York against the Red Sox. And while we've won up here this year, the Red Sox have won in Yankee Stadium."

When the Yankee and the Red Sox met a week later in New York, it was the Yanks who were in first place. They had won two of three from Detroit and had taken a 1½-game lead. The three-game series was crucial.

Lemon had his pitching rotation set. He had his ace, Guidry, ready for the opener against Tiant, Hunter against Torrez in the middle game, and finishing with Beattie against Eckersley. The Yankees were counting on taking two of the three games.

Guidry got them off in that direction. Once again he was magnificent. He blanked the Red Sox a second time, again spinning another two-hitter, 4–0. So unhittable was Guidry that the Red Sox batters managed to hit only five balls to the outfield.

Tiant, who wanted to pitch with only three days' rest the last time they played the Yankees, got his wish this time. Working with the shorter rest period, Tiant looked strong as he retired the first nine batters he faced. However, the Yanks broke loose in the fourth to score all their runs and send Tiant to an early shower. Chambliss and Nettles hit back-to-back homers to finish the Red Sox for the night.

"They're just not the same team they were in July earlier in the year," disclosed Guidry after winning his twenty-second game against only two defeats. "They're down, and they are getting on one another. They're not swinging freely. They're swinging at bad pitches, and they are not hitting some mistakes that I made."

When Hunter took the mound for the second game, the Yankees were 2½ games ahead of the Red Sox. This was Hunter's first appearance since he pulled a groin muscle against Boston more than a week ago. There were some doubts about how long he would last after the first inning. He gave up a single to Jerry Remy, and then Jim Rice poled his forty-first home run of the season to give Boston a quick 2–0 lead. It was the first time they led the Yanks in six games.

But Torrez couldn't handle Jackson. In the bottom of the first, Jackson singled home Willie Randolph for one run. Then in the fifth, Jackson tied the game at 2–2 by hitting an 0–2 pitch into the rightfield stands.

Meanwhile, Hunter settled down. He didn't experience any more difficulty until the ninth inning. But with two out, Hunter walked pinch-hitter Fred Lynn after opening the inning by walking Jack Brohamer. Lemon called time and walked to the mound to talk with Hunter as Rick Burleson approached the plate.

"How ya' feel, Meat?" inquired Lemon.

"Feel all right," answered Hunter. "Let me go after this guy."

"He's throwing pretty good, Skip," offered Munson.

"Okay, Meat, go on and get him," encouraged Lemon as he left the mound.

Hunter got Burleson on a fly ball to left-field. The Yankees now came up in the bottom of the ninth inning with Torrez facing the top of the order.

The ex-Yankee got two quick strikes on Rivers. Seeing Yastrzemski move in about 100 feet behind the shortstop, Rivers stepped out and swung on the next pitch. He drove the ball far over Yastrzemski's head. By the time the ball was returned to the infield, the speedy Rivers was on third base.

Torrez then got Randolph to ground out to shortstop in the drawn-in infield. Rivers couldn't run. Now Torrez had to face Munson. With the count at 1–1, Munson tried a suicide squeeze that went foul. However, on the very next pitch he drove a long fly to right-center where Rice made a diving catch. Rivers only had to trot home from third for the run that gave the Yankees an exciting 3–2 victory.

The Yankees had won the first two games. That's what they wanted, two victories. They now led the Red Sox by 3½ games. They felt more confident about winning the Eastern Division.

"This one could kill them," exclaimed Paul Blair. "They played well; they got good pitching, and we beat them anyway. They're hurting now. Can they come back? I'd say their chances are mighty slim."

Boston's slim hopes rested on the right arm of Dennis Eckersley. He was working on three days' rest. If the Red Sox won, they would cut the Yankee's margin to 2½ games. If the Red Sox lost, it would balloon the Yank edge to 4½ and practically finish off Boston.

But, Eckersley came through. He pitched a strong game for 6⅔ innings as the Red Sox stayed alive by beating the Yankees, 7–3. He and reliever Bob Stanley held the Yanks to only four hits. Yet, the Red Sox didn't seem overly happy with their victory.

"Every day you sit in front of your locker and ask God what the hell is going on," remarked Burleson. "And, of course, he doesn't give you an answer. It's hard to look people in the eye and explain. Maybe we just weren't as good as everybody thought."

But the Red Sox still clung to a strand of hope. Maybe in the waning two weeks of the season they could catch up.

"This was the most important game I've ever pitched," revealed Eckersley. "If we had lost, we're out of it. But we still have a problem. We can't do it ourselves. We need help. At least we're not out of it, and at least we did to them a little of what they did to us in

Graig Nettles

Boston. I still don't think, however, that the breaks have evened up.

"The victory changed our attitude, but it hasn't changed the situation that much. It's not out of the realm, I guess. The past is so incredible, so spectacular, so amazing. The future is very uncertain. How much can you say about the future?

"You hear the numbers, and it sounds like a pennant race. But if you'd lived through the past couple of weeks with us, you'd know that's a little misleading. It is a race, but we need some help. Maybe we're glad we don't have to play them anymore the way they dominated us."

The Yankees were still 2½ games in front.

They had only 14 games remaining while the Red Sox had 15. The loss didn't appear to hurt them at all.

"Naw, it won't hurt this club," offered Jackson. "This game was much bigger for them than it was for us. If they lose, they're just about out of it.

"Hey, look, you just don't go around sweeping Boston all the time. We did it to them last week, and we won the first two here. Sure, after you win the first two, you think sweep; but it doesn't quite work that way. Taking two out of three here has got to make us happier than a pig in slop."

The Yankees indeed felt good about things. They were delighted at the way they

NEW YORK YANKEES—Final Unofficial Games Played 163

THRU 10-02-78

Batter	PCT	G	AB	R	H	2B	3B	HR	RBI	BB	SO	SH	SF	HP	SB	CS	E
Alston	.000	3	3	0	0	0	0	0	0	0	2	0	0	0	0	0	0
Blair	.176	74	125	10	22	5	0	2	13	9	17	2	0	0	1	1	2
Chambliss	.274	162	625	81	171	26	3	12	90	41	60	1	6	5	2	1	4
Dent	.243	123	379	40	92	11	1	5	40	23	24	6	5	2	3	1	10
Doyle	.192	39	52	6	10	0	0	0	0	0	3	2	0	0	0	3	1
Garcia	.195	18	41	5	8	0	0	0	1	2	6	0	1	0	1	0	4
Healy	.000	1	1	0	0	0	0	0	0	0	1	0	0	0	0	0	0
Heath	.228	33	92	6	21	3	1	0	8	4	9	1	1	1	0	0	5
Jackson	.274	139	511	82	140	13	5	27	97	58	133	0	3	9	14	11	3
Johnson	.184	76	174	20	32	9	1	6	19	30	32	0	0	1	0	0	2
Johnstone	.262	36	65	6	17	0	0	1	6	4	10	0	1	3	0	2	0
Klutts	1.000	1	2	1	2	1	0	0	0	0	0	0	0	1	0	0	1
Munson	.297	154	617	73	183	27	1	6	71	35	71	1	10	3	2	3	11
Nettles	.276	159	587	81	162	23	2	27	93	59	69	1	9	6	1	1	11
Piniella	.314	130	472	67	148	34	5	6	69	34	35	4	1	2	3	1	7
Ramos	.000	1	0	0	0	0	0	0	0	0	0	0	0	0	0	0	0
Randolph	.279	134	499	87	139	18	6	3	42	82	51	6	5	4	36	7	16
Rivers	.265	141	559	78	148	25	8	11	48	29	51	7	6	3	25	5	8
Sherrill	.000	2	1	1	0	0	0	0	0	0	1	0	0	0	0	0	0
Spencer	.227	71	150	12	34	9	1	7	24	15	32	0	1	0	0	1	0
Stanley	.219	80	160	14	35	7	0	1	9	25	31	4	0	0	0	0	9
Thomasson	.276	51	116	20	32	4	1	3	20	13	22	0	1	0	0	2	3
Thomasson ..T	.233	98	270	37	63	8	2	8	36	28	66	2	1	0	4	3	7
White L	.244		180	26	44	7	1	6	24	29	24	0	0	1	8	3	1
White ...... R	.295		166	18	49	6	2	2	19	13	11	2	3	1	2	1	0
White ...... T	.269	103	346	44	93	13	3	8	43	42	35	2	3	2	10	4	1
Zeber L	.000		1	0	0	0	0	0	0	0	0	0	0	0	0	0	0
Zeber .... R	.000		5	0	0	0	0	0	0	0	0	0	0	0	0	0	1
Beattie	.000	25	0	0	0	0	0	0	0	0	0	0	0	0	0	0	3
Clay	.000	28	0	0	0	0	0	0	0	0	0	0	0	0	0	0	2
Davis	.000	4	0	0	0	0	0	0	0	0	0	0	0	0	0	0	0
Eastwick	.000	8	0	0	0	0	0	0	0	0	0	0	0	0	0	0	0
Figueroa	.000	35	0	0	0	0	0	0	0	0	0	0	0	0	0	0	1
Gossage	.000	63	0	0	0	0	0	0	0	0	0	0	0	0	0	0	3
Guidry	.000	37	0	1	0	0	0	0	0	0	0	0	0	0	0	0	2
Gullett	.000	8	0	0	0	0	0	0	0	0	0	0	0	0	0	0	0
Holtzman	.000	5	0	0	0	0	0	0	0	0	0	0	0	0	0	0	0
Hunter	.000	21	0	0	0	0	0	0	0	0	0	0	0	0	0	0	0
Kammeyer	.000	7	0	0	0	0	0	0	0	0	0	0	0	0	0	0	0
Lindblad	.000	7	0	0	0	0	0	0	0	0	0	0	0	0	0	0	0
Lyle	.000	59	0	0	0	0	0	0	0	0	0	0	0	0	0	0	1
McCall	.000	5	0	0	0	0	0	0	0	0	0	0	0	0	0	0	0
Messersmith	.000	6	0	0	0	0	0	0	0	0	0	0	0	0	0	0	0
Rajsich	.000	4	0	0	0	0	0	0	0	0	0	0	0	0	0	0	0
Tidrow	.000	31	0	0	0	0	0	0	0	0	0	0	0	0	0	0	0
DH Hitters	.256		598	70	153	30	5	21	93	62	116	1	3	5	7	3	0
PH Hitters	.258		97	16	25	4	0	3	21	9	19	0	1	1	0	0	0
Totals	.267		5583	735	1489	228	38	125	693	505	695	37	53	42	98	43	113

NEW YORK YANKEES—Final Unofficial Games Played 163

Pitcher	ERA	W	L	AP	GS	CG	SV	SHO	IP	H	R	ER	HR	BB	SO	HB	WP
Beattie	3.73	6	9	25	22	0	0	0	128.0	123	60	53	8	51	65	8	8
Clay	4.28	3	4	28	6	0	0	0	75.2	89	41	36	3	21	32	2	4
Davis	11.57	0	0	4	0	0	0	0	2.1	3	4	3	0	3	0	0	0
Eastwick	3.28	2	1	8	0	0	0	0	24.2	22	9	9	2	4	13	1	0
Figueroa	2.99	20	9	35	35	12	0	2	253.0	233	96	84	22	77	92	3	6
Gossage	2.01	10	11	63	0	0	27	0	134.1	87	41	30	9	59	122	2	5
Guidry	1.74	25	3	35	35	16	0	9	273.2	187	61	53	13	72	248	1	7
Gullett	3.63	4	2	8	8	2	0	0	44.2	46	19	18	3	20	28	1	1
Holtzman	4.08	1	0	5	3	0	0	0	17.2	21	8	8	2	9	3	0	0
Hunter	3.58	12	6	21	20	5	0	1	118.0	98	49	47	16	35	56	1	2
Kammeyer ...	5.82	0	0	7	0	0	0	0	21.2	24	15	14	1	6	11	2	0
Lindblad	4.42	0	0	7	1	0	0	0	18.1	21	9	9	4	8	9	0	1
Lindblad ....T	3.88	1	1	25	1	0	2	0	58.0	62	25	25	6	23	34	2	3
Lyle	3.47	9	3	59	0	0	9	0	111.2	116	46	43	6	33	33	4	1
McCall	5.62	1	1	5	1	0	0	0	16.0	20	10	10	2	6	7	1	3
Messersmith ..	5.64	0	3	6	5	0	0	0	22.1	24	21	14	7	15	16	1	3
Rajsich	4.05	0	0	4	2	0	0	0	13.1	16	6	6	0	6	9	0	0
Tidrow	3.84	7	11	31	25	4	0	0	185.1	191	87	79	13	53	73	5	5
Totals	3.18	100	63	351	163	39	36	16	1460.2	1321	582	516	111	478	817	32	43

VS A.L. EAST HOME ROAD TOTAL

	HOME W	HOME L	ROAD W	ROAD L	TOTAL W	TOTAL L
Baltimore	3	4	6	2	9	6
Boston	3	4	6	3	9	7
Cleveland	6	2	3	4	9	6
Detroit	6	2	5	2	11	4
Milwaukee	5	3	0	7	5	10
New York	0	0	0	0	0	0
Toronto	6	1	5	3	11	4
TOTALS	29	16	25	21	54	37

VS A.L. WEST HOME ROAD TOTAL

	HOME W	HOME L	ROAD W	ROAD L	TOTAL W	TOTAL L
California	3	2	2	3	5	5
Chicago	4	1	5	0	9	1
Kansas City	3	3	2	3	5	6
Minnesota	3	2	4	1	7	3
Oakland	5	0	3	2	8	2
Seattle	4	1	2	4	6	5
Texas	4	1	2	3	6	4
TOTALS	26	10	20	16	46	26
GRAND TOT	55	26	45	37	100	63

1978 SEASON TOTALS

	NY	OPP
Errors	113	132
Double Play	135	150
Comp Games	39	41
Stolen Base	98	83
Caught Stlg	43	61
Doubles	228	249
Triples	38	38
Homers-Home	68	59
Homers-Road	57	52
Homers-Tot	125	111
Lf on Base	1153	1098

	W	L
Day	29	26
Night	71	37
Sho-Indv	12	6
Sho-Team	16	7
1-Run Gm	24	18
2-Run Gm	24	11
Extra Inn	7	6
vs Right	49	31
vs Left	51	32
Dbl-Hdr	3	1
Split	4	
Starters	77	43
Relief	23	20
Streaks	7	4

ATTENDANCE

	HOME	ROAD
Total	2335871	2063776
Ave.	30735	26124
Dates	76	79
Games	81	82

turned the season around. Some looked back and didn't mind giving the reasons why.

"It takes two things," said Lemon. "One, you have to be healthy, and two, the other team has to come back to you. Then, all of a sudden, everybody picks up 20 points in the batting average, and the pitching came around. At about the time I came here, everybody was just about healthy again, which Billy hadn't had. This club knows how to win; they're world champions. They can cope with adversity. They don't think negatively. We were lucky to catch Boston when they were having problems. We go to Boston hoping to win two of four and end up sweeping."

"It's very simple," offered Nettles. "We just got a set lineup together. Some people look for the manager and a different attitude on the club. Some of the guys were not comfortable with Billy. I was. We just got over the injuries. When the middle of the field came back, we started to win. I said the only way we could catch the Red Sox was if they went into a slump. We could have played the best baseball in the world and still not caught them."

"I feel like the pitching carried us back," said Rivers. "Some problems were taken care of, and we went back to work. We couldn't go no way but up. I guess the guys want to win. If you want to win bad enough, you can go out and do a job. We'd have done it with anybody up there managing."

"First of all, talent," claimed Jackson. "And a lot of tension in the clubhouse has been relieved since Billy's been gone. I was tired of it. Lemon's low-keyedness is what the club needed at that time. I'm sure that there were times when Billy's way was needed in the past. Catfish being better makes Nettles and Jackson hit better. It's not easy to hit when you're four runs down.

"We wouldn't have had to come from so far behind if we hadn't been hurt. When this club has nine healthy players and four healthy pitchers, it's not going to lose too many. In the two years I've spent on this club, when the time comes, these guys wake up and start playing ball. Other teams know it's going to be coming. At this time of year, you're going to get more tired mentally when every ball to you seems to mean a game. This team plays under tension every day. At least we did, so what's another pressure day? The main thing Lemon did was to come in and drop all the outside baloney tension. When you can concentrate on baseball, you're going to play it better."

"When good players get healthy, they win," pointed out Chris Chambliss. "It seems like they can turn it on when they feel like it, like a spigot; but it doesn't work that way. You have to push all the time and hope it works. If we win, I'll be happy. I won't be surprised. Injuries were a part of everything. When you got starting pitching, the runs start to mean something. Lemon being here is just fate, as it turned out, after being fired in Chicago. Billy's own problems came to a head and became the team's problems. Billy's interests were the team's; and when he knew it was hard for the team to endure the problems he had, he stepped out. Champions come back. That's what it's all about."

"We came back probably because we had something to prove," added Guidry, "that we were not the club we seemed to be. We lacked a lot of unity for a long time. Sometimes when we walked in the clubhouse there was something in the air that could explode any minute. We don't have that now. Lemon left everybody alone. He said, 'hello' and 'goodbye' and 'we'll get them tomorrow.'"

"It's very simple," said Piniella. "We just

got the best team in the league. When we were behind, we were playing with a makeshift lineup. This club plays better with the pressure on. We've proved that over the last couple of years. I knew we had a chance when the Red Sox took that big lead, and it came back to 6½ fairly quickly. Lemon has been a strong influence. There's been no bitching or serious problems with him. The players were tired of the bickering; we had it for so long. He lets us play baseball. The biggest thing Lemon did was the way he handled the pitching. Rosen has been a steadying influence. He hasn't meddled, and Steinbrenner seems to have confidence in his judgment."

Yet, two weeks of the regular season remained. The Yankees still had to go about the task of locking up the Eastern Division race. In the first week, they hit a bad spell. They lost four of seven games and tenaciously clung to a one-game lead. Then they got hot again. They won six games in a row. But Boston, too, kept winning. Amazingly, they kept pace with the Yankees. The race was going down to the final day of the season, one game separating the two clubs.

The Red Sox got some unexpected help. After the Yanks had left Cleveland for dead, beating them in the first two games of a three-game set at Yankee Stadium, the Indians fought back. They routed Hunter on the final game of the season, 9–2, while the Red Sox beat the Detroit Tigers. The Yanks and Red Sox finished the season in a tie with 99–63 records. They were even now.

The Yanks had to go to Boston for one more game, a sudden death playoff . . .

8

Playoff Game

The drama continued. It seemed as if it would never end. The whole season had come down to one game. There wouldn't be any tomorrows for either the Yankees or the Red Sox. All season long they had been at each other's throats. The Yankees kept scratching and clawing until they overcame a 14-game handicap. All they had had to do was to beat Cleveland in the final game of the season and it would have been all over. But they didn't. The Red Sox got a life. After 162 regular season games, the Yankees and Red Sox were even. All that remained was a one-game playoff to determine the winner of the Eastern Division.

Bob Lemon did a strange thing after his team lost to Cleveland on the final Sunday of the regular season. He closed the doors to the Yankee clubhouse and quietly talked to his players. He stood among them for about 20 minutes and talked in that easy way of his. No shouting or yelling. Just a calming effect

that enabled his players to think about tomorrow and their sudden death meeting in Boston.

"Lem closed the door, sat us down, and told us something," disclosed reserve first baseman Jim Spencer. "He told us if he never got another chance, he was proud of us. He told us, 'Thanks for putting out and for making such a great comeback in the second half.' He told us, 'One more game,' and that if everybody put out, we'd win it. He did it, he said, in case he didn't get a chance to do it later."

It was a Sunday of meetings. Before the Yankees took the field against the Indians, they assembled in Lemon's office for their regular Sabbath chapel meeting. Most of the players attended, about 20 of them. It wasn't a formal prayer meeting. Rather, it offered the players a quiet moment to meditate.

The guest speaker was a tall bearded individual named Tom Skinner. He left the players with something different to think about, something along the lines of faith and humility.

"I want to talk to you about this man Job in the Old Testament," began Skinner. "But, so you'll better understand, I'm going to bring him into the modern scene. We'll call him J.B.

"Now J.B. has everything anyone could ask for, a big 20-room house in Westchester, a dozen servants, big limousine. He had wealth, prestige, and power. He also was a man of God. You also have wealth, prestige, and power. You are in the top 1½ percent of the nation's income bracket. People look to you for example.

"Just remember this. You had to adjust to God's agenda. He will not adjust to yours. Now take J.B. One day he gets a phone call. Someone tells him that all his children are dead. J.B. is shaken but replies, 'Praise the Lord.' What do you mean, 'Praise the Lord?' the caller asked. 'I said all your children are dead.' 'I know,' J.B. said. 'God gave them to me and now he has taken them back.'

"One day J.B. drives his limousine down Bruckner Boulevard to his office. His directors are waiting for him. They tell him the stock market has crashed, the banks have gone broke, all of his companies are bankrupt, his factories are burning down. 'Praise the Lord,' said J.B.''

It might have been a bit heavy. A few minutes later the Yankees took the field against the Indians. They weren't exactly a symbol of power in falling before the Indians, 9-2.

"It's like the man told us in the chapel meeting before the game, we don't control our destiny," remarked Jackson. "If it's God's will, that's the way it has to be. You gotta remember, the Indians are God's children, too, and they flat out whipped us good.

"It's a damn shame that we and the Red Sox both have to be in the same division, but that's the way it goes. I personally believe that the winner of the game will be the best team. But then again, I don't care who the best team is. I just want to win it."

The oddsmakers didn't figure that the Yanks would win it. They established the Red Sox as favorites, and for a number of reasons, too. For one thing, and a very important one, the Red Sox were playing at home. And through the years the Red Sox have proven extremely difficult to beat in the friendly confines of Fenway Park. The small ball park has always been a hitter's paradise and a pitcher's nightmare, especially for left-handers.

And the Yankees had a left-hander going, Guidry. Although he was the best pitcher in baseball with an amazing 24–3 record, the oddsmakers felt it wasn't enough against Boston's powerful lineup. They also made an important point in emphasizing that Guidry was working with only three days' rest. They were aware that he is much more effective with the normal four days' rest and that he worked with only three days between starts only three times all season. Still, it didn't bother Guidry in the least.

"So I pitch with three days' rest? So what?" snapped Guidry. "I think I know what to do about it. If my arm is live, or livelier, I'll know what to do. I think I've learned about pitching, and with Munson calling the pitches, it all has a meaning. Things have been pretty good so far. We've been working on a good thing. Why change anything?"

One of the good things was that Guidry had complete control of the Red Sox. In the last two games he pitched against them, he was overpowering. He hurled back-to-back, two-hit shutouts which nobody had ever done to the Red Sox. And, if Guidry couldn't go the entire way, there was always Gossage, the best reliever in baseball, behind him.

"I'm ready and strong," remarked Gossage. "I'll go as long as I have to. Because it's only one game. I personally don't believe the winner will be the better team. We're both so damn close when it comes to talent, but I think we have more. I also like our chances."

Another reason the oddsmakers didn't like the Yankees' chances was the fact that second baseman Willie Randolph was hurt and definitely wouldn't play. Besides being an excellent fielder, he is also a fine hitter, one that batted second in the lineup behind

Mickey Rivers. With Randolph sidelined, it meant that the Yanks would have to start Brian Doyle at second base. Doyle is a good fielder, but his hitting was glaringly weaker than Randolph's. As a result, Lemon had to insert Doyle in the eighth spot in the batting order just ahead of shortstop Bucky Dent. Offensively, the Yanks were a bit weaker with this arrangement.

Ironically, Boston manager Don Zimmer selected Mike Torrez to face the Yanks. The big right-hander was with the Yankees the year before, winning 14 games and then hurling two victories in the World Series. However, he elected not to re-sign with the Yankees but became a free agent and signed a $2.6 million, multi-year contract with Boston.

After a strong start at the beginning of the season, Torrez began to lose in the second half. He had won only one game since August 18, and it came in his last start against the Detroit Tigers. He appeared strong in allowing the Tigers only three hits in a 1–0 shutout.

Like Guidry, he, too, was working on only three days' rest. But that's the way he prefers it. He faced the Yanks three times during the season and was beaten twice. The Red Sox were hoping that Torrez would continue where he left off against the Tigers.

"We got what we were hoping for; now let's see what we can do," exclaimed Torrez. "We've been playing super, and I'm just happy to get the chance. Now we have the chance, and we are all looking forward to it. I know those guys over there, and you can be sure I'll be giving it my best shot."

It was only the second playoff game in the history of the American League. The first one occurred 30 years before, and ironically, the game involved the Red Sox. Again the scene was Boston, and the Red Sox lost the opportunity to play in the 1948 World Series by losing to the Cleveland Indians in an exciting game.

One game was all that was left. The possibilities of it being exciting were strong. After all, two heated rivals, perhaps the two best teams in baseball, were facing each other in a one-game shoot-out. The players on both sides well knew the importance of the game. After all, there was no tomorrow.

"If we win, then the better team will have won it," reasoned Graig Nettles. "But honestly, the team that wins shouldn't be considered the better team. We're so evenly matched. I just hope it's not a conservatively played game. I'd like to keep playing the kind of ball we've been playing."

Partisan Red Sox fans elbowed their way into Fenway Park on a beautiful fall afternoon. Only 32,925 of them could be accommodated in the tiny stadium which was the smallest in either league.

It was an antiquated yet historic stadium. Boston had been a member of the American League since 1901. Through the years, the Red Sox had produced such legendary stars as Cy Young, Babe Ruth, Ted Williams, Jimmy Foxx, and Carl Yastrzemski. Almost as famous was its short leftfield wall that was only 315 feet from home plate. It was known as the Green Monster because it devoured more than one visiting pitcher.

Yastrzemski was its guardian. The veteran 39-year-old star had played most of his 18 years with the Red Sox in leftfield. It's like an eternity. Yaz knows every inch of the wall and the ground below it. It has come to be known as "Yaz's Little Acre." Nobody, but nobody, can play the area better than Yastrzemski. While pitchers envision the wall as a monster, Yaz looks upon it as an ally.

There is no counting the number of baseballs Yaz has seen bouncing off the wall. In 18 years, it has gone far beyond the bounds of calculation. But what Yaz has done during all those years is make a scientific study of how the balls ricochet off the green concrete 37 feet in height. Every batter who comes to Fenway takes aim at the wall.

Yastrzemski's teammate Jim Rice always swings in the direction of the wall, and with good reason. There is no better right-handed hitting slugger in baseball than Rice, who led both leagues in home runs with 46. His swing is awesome. In a close game, he could make the difference.

But it was Yastrzemski who got the Red Sox

going. Leading off the second inning, he caught hold of a Guidry fastball and drove it into the seats for a 1–0 Boston lead. Then, in the sixth inning, Rice lined a sharp single to drive in Boston's second run.

Trailing 2–0, the Yanks had a rally going in the seventh inning. With one out, Chambliss and White hit consecutive singles. But Jim Spencer, pinch-hitting for Brian Doyle, popped out. That left it up to Dent. There were many who thought that Lemon would lift his light-hitting shortstop for a pinch-hitter. But Lemon was out of reserve infielders, and Dent had to bat for himself.

He took a ball and then fouled the next pitch from Torrez off his foot. He hobbled around in pain before he stepped back into the batter's box. Torrez quickly fired the next pitch, and Dent swung. He sent the ball deep into leftfield, high and far toward the wall. A few seconds later, Yastrzemski looked up and saw the ball clear the wall for a three-run homer that gave the Yanks a 3–2 lead.

Shaken by the blow, Torrez then walked Rivers. Zimmer then signaled for Bob Stanley to relieve Torrez. The first batter he faced was Munson, and the Yankee catcher drove a drive into left-center for a double that scored Rivers and increased the Yanks' edge to 4–2.

Guidry struck out Butch Hobson to start off the bottom of the seventh. However, George Scott smacked a single, and Lemon called in Gossage to relieve Guidry. The ace reliever retired the Red Sox without any further trouble.

The Yanks weren't finished. Jackson led off the eighth inning with a home run to give the Yanks a 5–2 lead. It proved to be the margin of victory as the Red Sox rallied for two runs in their turn at bat to cut their deficit to 5–4. That's the way it ended, despite some dramatic moments in the bottom of the ninth when Yastrzemski fouled out to end the game with two runners on base. The Yankees had won the Eastern Division championship in the one-hundred-sixty-third game of the season. The entire 162-game season came down to a sudden death playoff game.

It was a deliriously happy Yankee club-house. Perhaps more joyous than in the preceding year. The long, uphill climb of the Yankees bordered on a miracle. No other team in the history of the American League ever came from so far behind as 14 games to win a championship. And it all came down to a sudden death game with an unlikely hero in light-hitting Bucky Dent, who went unnoticed as the ninth batter in the lineup.

The night before the game, owner George Steinbrenner did happen to notice something about Dent. He talked to his plucky shortstop and noticed that he was a bit down in spirits.

"Bucky was a little down in the mouth," disclosed Steinbrenner. "Last night I showed him a piece of paper I had and told him that he was hitting .140 over the last 20 games but that he shouldn't let that discourage him. I told him that he was overdue and that he would snap out of it. You saw the way he did it, didn't you?

"In fact, Al Rosen called Bucky's home run before he hit it. He said, 'He's gonna hit one out,' and sure enough, he did. It couldn't happen to a finer young man."

The way it happened was unbelievable. Dent and Rivers were sharing a Roy White model bat during the game. But the first time that Rivers got up, he noticed that there was a slight crack in the bat. Rivers switched bats after that, but Dent kept using the White model.

When time was called in the seventh inning after Dent hurt his foot while at bat, Rivers walked over to him with a bat in his hands. He was in the on-deck circle waiting his turn to hit next.

"Here, Bucky, here," yelled Rivers. "Gimme that bat. Take this one."

The Yankees' date with destiny was actually realized with a borrowed bat in the hands of a soft-hitting shortstop who was in a slump. And to add further to the drama, the manager couldn't pinch-hit for him because there wasn't anybody around who could play shortstop.

"I knew we didn't have another short-stop," smiled Dent. "I went up the plate thinking that here's my chance to show

Bucky Dent hits a three-run homer off Mike Torres of the Red Sox in the seventh inning of the playoff game. (Wide World Photos)

Bucky Dent is greeted by Bob Lemon and Cliff Johnson after the three-run homer. (Wide World Photos)

them. I was just going up trying to make contact.

"After I fouled the pitch off my ankle and the trainer came out to look at it, Mickey Rivers hollered to me that I had a crack in the bat and to take his. You really couldn't tell that there was anything wrong with the bat. It was all taped up. Mickey's bat was an M-44 Model that he had stuck in the bottom of the bat bag. When I hit the homer I wasn't sure if it was going out, and I didn't even look at it until after I had gotten to first base. I thought the best it could do was hit the wall. I didn't know it cleared the wall until after I was past first base.

"I'll tell you, though, when those guys came up in the bottom of the ninth, Rice and Yastrzemski, I could feel the sweat trickling down my back. Rice has done it all year and Yaz all day, heck, all his career."

But destiny made Dent the hero, a little guy with a big hit. It was David and Goliath all over again. Even Jackson, who gave the Yanks what turned out to be the insurance run with a homer of his own in the very next inning, smiled at Dent.

"The big guy, he hit one," beamed Jackson. "Before Bucky came up, I turned to Catfish Hunter alongside of me and said to him, 'I just would like Bucky to hit the tins.' All I wanted was for Bucky to drive in the two men on base and tie the game. I wasn't asking for a home run.

"The ball I hit was a fastball. When it wound up in the bleachers, I just thought it was an extra run. I just feel good that we won, and what makes it so wonderful is that it was a collective victory. We all had a hand in it. But I didn't want it to end up 5-4. That put too much pressure on us."

The pressure was all on the shoulders of Gossage. He wasn't as overpowering as he usually is. In the 2⅔ innings he worked, he allowed two runs, five hits, and struck out only two batters. But when he needed the big pitch, he had it. He got the dangerous Yastrzemski out with one of his blinding fastballs to seal the victory. And he did it dramatically. Not only was the tying run on third base, but the potential winner was also on first base. It was high drama, indeed.

"I knew I had my hands full," admitted Gossage. "They're great fastball hitters. They know I'm not a breaking-ball pitcher, so something's got to give. It was power against power. My mind flashed back to my home in the Rockies. The worst thing that could happen is that I couldn't go spend my winter there. It's a beautiful place, and it's a way to take a little of the pressure off. Every ballplayer, every athlete, has his manner of relaxing. Crazy things go through your head. It's not all baseball.

"Worried wasn't exactly the way I felt. You don't have time to think of situations when you're in a position like that. I made up my mind that if I was going to get beat, I would get beat with my best pitch, the fastball. And that was what he hit for the final out. I threw a fastball that tailed inside. I got it where I wanted it. I saw the ball go into the air and Nettles get under it. I can't tell you how it made me feel."

It certainly made Lemon feel good. He used his two best pitchers against the heavy-hitting Red Sox and came away winning. He admitted that he went with his heart in deciding to replace Guidry with Gossage in the seventh inning. He also disclosed that he couldn't even remember what he said to Gossage when he went out to the mound and talked to him in the final inning.

"I don't even know what the hell I said to him," said Lemon, shaking his head. "But there was no way I was taking him out. He's the best I got. Listen, anytime you keep the ball inside this ball park, you're doing something.

"And I went about as long as I could with my other guy. There was no way I was going to let him take a loss today, not after what he's meant to us. After we got ahead, Guidry wasn't going to lose it. I made up my mind on that. Why not go with fresh meat? When I took him out, he said, 'Good luck.' If they're all like that, you'd never have a problem."

Lemon made a tough decision, but nevertheless a wise one. It's difficult to remove

PLAYOFF GAME STATISTICS

NEW YORK	AB	R	H	BI	BOSTON	AB	R	H	BI
Rivers CF	2	1	1	0	Burleson SS	4	1	1	0
Blair CF	1	0	1	0	Remy 2B	4	1	2	0
Munson C	5	0	1	1	Rice RF	5	0	1	1
Piniella RF	4	0	1	0	Yastrzemski LF	5	2	2	2
Jackson DH	4	1	1	1	Fisk C	3	0	1	0
Nettles 3B	4	0	0	0	Lynn CF	4	0	1	1
Chambliss 1B	4	1	1	0	Hobson DH	4	0	1	0
White LF	3	1	1	0	Scott 1B	4	0	2	0
Thomasson LF	0	0	0	0	Brohamer 3B	1	0	0	0
Doyle 2B	2	0	0	0	Bailey PH	1	0	0	0
Spencer PH	1	0	0	0	Duffy 3B	0	0	0	0
Stanley 2B	1	0	0	0	Evans PH	1	0	0	0
Dent SS	4	1	1	3	Torrez P	0	0	0	0
Guidry P	0	0	0	0	Stanley P	0	0	0	0
Gossage P	0	0	0	0	Hassler P	0	0	0	0
					Drago P	0	0	0	0
Totals	35	5	8	5	Totals	36	4	11	4

Yankees—0 0 0 0 0 0 4 1 0—5 8 0
Boston —0 1 0 0 0 1 0 2 0—4 11 0
  LOB—Yankees 6, Boston 9. 2B—Rivers, Munson, Scott, Burleson, Remy. HR—Dent (5), Yastrzemski (17), Jackson (27). SB—Rivers 2 S—Brohamer, Remy.

	IP	H	R	ER	BB	SO
Guidry (W 25-3)	6 1-3	6	2	2	1	5
Gossage	2 2-3	5	2	2	1	2
Torrez (L 16-13)	6 2-3	5	4	4	3	4
Stanley	1-3	2	1	1	0	0
Hassler	1 2-3	1	0	0	0	2
Drago	1-3	0	0	0	0	0

  Stanley pitched to 1 batter in 8th.
  Save—Gossage (27). PB—Munson. T—2:52. A—32,925.

your ace in the late innings after your team has finally gone ahead by two runs. But after Butch Hobson struck out opening the bottom of the seventh, George Scott lined a single. That's when Lemon decided to relieve Guidry.

"I didn't want to come out," admitted Guidry. "I was pretty strong for the first three innings. Then I guess I was down to 80 percent. I've pitched better games, but not many that were as important. So even though I wasn't that effective, I'm still very pleased.

"I really don't think that pitching on the fourth day is for me. I'm strong for a few innings, and then I lose something. But this situation you can't have what you want. I knew I wasn't going to be overpowering, but I wanted to keep us close. If they score one or two, that's only natural because they're a great club and they're in their park.

"I know Lem was thinking of me. I've had a great season, and he didn't want to see it tainted. But no other person has come through it but me, and I felt I should win it or lose it. I wasn't really happy about coming out. But I also understand he makes the decision. Lemon could tell I was getting tired. He's the boss.

"From that point on I couldn't do anything but root. Bucky was in a slump, 0 for 20 or something like that, when he came up. It was going to be one of his last times up. Why not go for the full pump? You've got a short porch. When you're in a slump, you hit line drives, and they are caught. No one in the world can jump high enough to catch the one Bucky hit. I'm glad it was him."

So was Lemon. He was in a spot. He confided that he wanted to pinch-hit for Dent at that moment, but couldn't.

"If I didn't need Stanley to replace Doyle at second base, I would have pinch-hit for Dent," admitted Lemon. "That shows you how much I know."

While Dent's home run might have won it, a great many of the players felt that it was Piniella's play in rightfield in the ninth inning that saved the precious victory for the Yankees. In late afternoon, Fenway's rightfield is the worst sun field in the majors. Yet, Piniella made two great plays half-blinded by the wretched sun. He held one ball, hit by Jerry Remy, to a single and then made a circus catch of a long drive by Jim Rice.

For an instant, Piniella saw both balls that were hit. However, he lost them in the glare of the sun. Remy's hit fell about seven feet in front of him, yet he managed to decoy the batter into thinking he would catch the ball, which forced Rick Burleson into holding up near first base.

"Sure, I catch it if I see it," explained Piniella about Remy's single. "But the way it was with the sun so low, it could have hit me anywhere, in the stomach, chest, anywhere. You've just got to keep watching, hoping you'll pick it up. You can't panic because then you let the runner know you're not catching the ball and he's sure to go to third.

"I saw the ball come off the bat, but I didn't see anything after that. But I moved back three or four feet hoping to keep the ball in front of me. I started pounding my glove like I was going to make the catch. If you start pounding your glove like you have it, then the runner can't go. I heard the ball

hit the ground, and I reached for it. I was lucky."

When Rice hit his ball toward rightfield, many thought it would land in the stands for a game-winning homer. Roy White, who was watching from leftfield, felt it would.

"When Rice's ball first left the bat, I thought it was going out. It left the bat fast, and I know how strong Rice is. I've seen him hit so many opposite field homers."

But Piniella knew it wouldn't carry far enough into the seats, even though he had difficulty following the ball. He just kept hoping he would get to see it at all and make the catch.

"I was trying to locate it through the sun," explained Piniella. "I knew the ball wasn't deep enough to go out. The ball scared the hell out of me for a minute because I couldn't see it and I was thinking, 'Oh, no, I'm not going to catch it and they're going to win the pennant.'"

Even the Red Sox felt that Piniella's outfield play was the turning point in the game. Some of them, in fact, pointed out the veteran rightfielder's catch of a line drive by Fred Lynn in the sixth inning that seemed certain to fall safely. Boston manager Don Zimmer for one. There were two outs and two runners on base at the time.

"No question about it," exclaimed Zimmer in the ghost-like quiet of the Boston clubhouse. "I was standing with Dwight Evans at the time. He told me that was the toughest part of the field and the toughest time of day. Anybody who says that Piniella can't play the outfield can go jump in the lake. I've never seen him make a mistake out there."

Neither did Yastrzemski. He also felt that Piniella's catch of Lynn's screaming drive down the rightfield line was the game saver.

"I don't know what he was doing playing Lynn that close to the line with Guidry throwing. Me, I could see because I pull the ball; but, especially against hard-throwing lefties, Freddie goes more straightaway or to the left. I don't know why he was playing there, but he was right."

It was a tough loss for Yastrzemski. More so than for anyone. In the twilight of a bril-

Graig Nettles

liant career, he wanted one more try at the brass ring, one more chance to play in a World Series. He was so emotionally overcome that he cried. That said it all.

"All losses are tough," sighed Yastrzemski. "It's eating my guts out right now. But I'm going fishing for two weeks and then start breaking my back to get ready for next year. It just wasn't meant to be. But I'll tell you something. Yaz is gonna be on a world champion before he retires from this club. There's just too much talent on this club not to win it."

Yaz had a number of traumatic moments during the pulsating struggle. One gave him joy, the home run he hit in the second inning off Guidry, the best pitcher in baseball, to give Boston a 1–0 lead. The others gave him anguish. The first was when he stood and watched Dent's home run land in the screen in the seventh inning. The other was making the final out of the game with the tying run on third base and the winning run on first. It was hard for even a veteran like Yastrzemski to endure, and his tears showed it.

"At first I didn't think Dent's ball would make it," remarked Yaz. "When the ball went into the net, my insides dropped out of me. I felt bad for the club, for the fans, and for Torrez, who had pitched such a fine game until then.

"I was looking for a fastball from Gossage the last time up. But Gossage has the kind of fastball that moves. Not like Nolan Ryan's. It came in, and I did just what I wanted to, but it ran in and I was jammed.

"My insides are all knots. I don't have words to express how I feel. I know we're a helluva ball club, and there's nothing any player has to be ashamed about. Sometimes you wonder if it was meant to be or not."

Burleson wondered about it, too. He felt that fate played a role in not enabling the Red Sox to win the division championship.

"There's got to be fate involved," expressed Burleson as he was searching for answers. "Piniella didn't see the fly ball Remy hit in the ninth and yet it bounced up and hit his glove. I was on first base at the time, and yet I couldn't take a chance and run in case he caught the ball; but then I saw the expression on his face like he couldn't see the ball. It fell, but I couldn't take a chance of going to third.

"He doesn't see the ball, and it bounced into his glove. We weren't supposed to win. When we were ahead 2–0, I was confident that we were going to the playoffs. Then came the three-run homer by Dent, and Jackson's homer turns out to be the game-winner.

"It's a sad ending as far as I am concerned. I thought we had it, but that guy up in the sky has something to do with it. No matter how far we were ahead, we were not going to win."

It was hard for Burleson to speak. It was also hard for the rest of the players. Most of them stood alone, trying to put it all together on what really happened, coming to grips with the reality that it was all over. Quietly, with shallow voices, they spoke.

"I tried my best," hesitated Torrez, "but when Dent hit the ball I thought it was either an out or off the wall. I never thought it would make the screen. I threw him a fastball in, just about where I wanted it. What can I say? It's hard to explain. I felt comfortable, was able to change speeds and put the ball where I wanted to.

"You have to give the Yankees credit. They're a great club. We tried our best but came up one run short. I know in my heart I gave it the best I could, and the team played its heart out. We came back from 5–2, and Remy hit that ball that Piniella knocked down which would have won it for us. But it just didn't happen that way.

"We all busted our butts. We didn't fold. We wanted this badly. I'm sorry we didn't come out on top, but there only can be one winner."

That's the way the Yankees felt, too. They were gracious winners. Several came into the Red Sox clubhouse and talked to the players. An hour before, they had been bitter rivals, playing for a title that only one could win. The two teams were separated by only one run. That's what the entire season came down to, a single run in a playoff game. It was over.

"I honestly don't know who the best team is," remarked Jackson as he went around talking to Rice, Fisk, and Scott, among others. "Either of these teams would be representative. You guys would be even better against a left-handed pitcher.

"It's a shame they can't go with us. They're a super ball club. They're just as good as we are. What we did today shows how close we are. The one-hundred-sixty-third game, 5–4 with a man on third in the ninth. Either team could have won. The Red Sox didn't lose. We won.

"Fisk, you're a superstar. I love to watch you play, but I hate to play against you. Rice, you had the strongest offensive year I've ever seen and deserve to be in the playoffs. You know as much about the outfield as I do. But, hey, if we weren't doing this, we'd be driving trucks."

The only one who was driving anywhere was Zimmer. Red-eyed and exhausted, he was scheduled to drive to his Florida home the next day.

"People who watch the playoffs and World Series will suffer a letdown," offered Zimmer. "That was one great ball game. I don't know how I'm going to take the 1,500 miles I have to drive. I know how I feel."

The Red Sox bags were lined up in the corridor, neatly stacked one on top of the other. They were earmarked for Kansas City if the Red Sox had won. Bill Lee, the colorful but controversial left-hander, walked by and glanced over at the pile.

"I guess this means we don't get to go anywhere," he remarked sadly.

The Yankees were going to Kansas City . . .

Lou Piniella

9

American League Championship

The Royals wanted revenge. They had met the Yankees in two previous championship playoffs and had lost both times. It was embarrassing. Now they were rested and waiting for the Yankees. They were determined not to let them win a third straight time. Their frustrations began to show the year before when the rival third basemen, Graig Nettles and George Brett, got involved in a brawl that brought players from both dugouts running onto the field. The Yanks-Royals rivalry was tense. Not as heated, perhaps, as the Yanks-Red Sox donnybrook, but nevertheless just behind in intensity.

Nettles remembered the altercation with Brett, but he didn't stay awake nights thinking about it.

"You remember that those things happen," remarked Nettles. "But you don't dwell on them. They're just the product of people playing very intensely. I don't expect there will be any carryover to these playoffs,

but I wouldn't be surprised if something similar happened because of the intensity of the playoffs."

The Royals were confident this time. There were many in baseball who felt they had an edge. Their optimism was based on three established facts. One, the Yankees were tired after their emotionally exhausting sudden death playoff against Boston the day before; two, the Yanks' pitching staff was disorganized since ace left-hander Ron Guidry had pitched against Boston with only two days' rest; and three, the first two games in the best-of-five playoffs were being played on the artificial turf of Royals Stadium where Kansas City set a club record by winning 56 of 81 games.

All the logic was sound. The Yankees' pitching rotation was so scrambled that Jim Beattie, with a 6–9 record, was named to open against Dennis Leonard, 21–17. The power-throwing Leonard had a 16–5 record at home, but the Yankees also inserted some logic.

"Anytime you start a series on the road, you plan on a split in the first two games," analyzed Piniella. "Anything else would be disastrous. But considering what we've been through and that we've had to play so hard in the last three weeks, I think I'd be more than pleased if we could win one of the games in Kansas City."

Lemon, too, weighed the facts. He saw things differently.

"I don't think any team gets too tired to play hard in the playoffs," remarked Lemon. "A team like the Royals might have an advantage because they clinched pretty early and got a chance to rest, but some people think it's a disadvantage because a team that rests for a long time can lose its fine edge. The team that's supposed to be so tired just might knock them off."

Yet, no one was more optimistic than Kansas City manager Whitey Herzog. While he had his best pitcher going in the opener, the Yanks could only counter with their number four man.

"It's a break for us that they can't open with Guidry," exclaimed Herzog. "Originally, I thought our chances of winning this playoff were bad if he could pitch the first and fifth games. But the most he'll be able to pitch now is one game, and that puts things in our favor. You can't say we couldn't beat him; but when a guy is 25–3, you know your chances aren't too good."

The Royals didn't feel too good after the first game was played. They were embarrassed, 7–1, as the Yanks slammed out 16 hits while Beattie and Ken Clay held the Royals to only two hits. They were stopped by two pitchers who had a combined won-lost record of 9–13!

Jackson led the 16-hit assault with a perfect night, going three for three. He had a single his first time up, a double in the third, and a three-run homer in the eighth. He also walked twice and scored three runs.

Leonard was stunned. He couldn't explain it. It was one of the hardest he was hit all year.

"I don't know what happened," sighed Leonard. "The fastballs started getting up, and they were hitting. I was struggling out there."

So were the rest of the Royals. They had no pitching and no hitting.

"The defense and the offense were just crap," moaned Brett. "I'm just glad it's over. Just a bad night. We thought we had a chance to win. Maybe we thought we had the first two games won already. And Beattie. I don't even know the guy's first name, but he's good. He proved it tonight." -

The only disappointment Beattie felt was in not pitching longer. He lasted 5⅓ innings and gave up both Kansas City hits. But he was happy, nevertheless.

"I wanted to get in seven innings, but we won," smiled Beattie. "I had some trouble getting the ball over, but Ken came in and did a good job. I enjoyed the situation. Being in the first game and having everybody count on you, it makes you feel you can do better."

The Yanks were assured of a split. That's what they were playing for. In the second game they had Ed Figueroa ready to face Larry Gura. Both pitchers had fine years, Figueroa 20–9 and Gura 16–4.

However, Figueroa didn't have it. He yielded a run in the first inning and was chased in the second as the Royals went on to an easy 10–4 victory to even the playoffs. What marked the Royals' win was that they played aggressively, almost too much so. Willie Wilson blasted Munson at home and cut his chin so badly that Munson required stitches after the game. Then Clint Hurdle slid so hard into Nettles at third base that he produced a throwing error that accounted for two early runs. Finally, reliever Al Hrabosky fired a couple of brush-back pitches that showed he meant business.

"Both teams are aggressive," pointed out Brett. "But we're both more aggressive against each other than anyone else. That's never going to cease. We've got too many memories of each other. Whenever a pitch comes by your chin, you think back and wonder, 'Let's see, what did I once do to this guy?'

Reggie Jackson

Reggie Jackson misses a long fly by the Royals' Clint Hurdle. It was a triple. (Wide World Photos)

"We've faced Figgy so often that we know him inside out," continued Brett, who went 13 for 13 against the Yankee right-hander one year. "When he drops sidearm, it's a slider. Overhand, it's either the fastball or curve. We were just flat embarrassed after the first game."

The Yankees were a little concerned about Munson. He had taken the full force of White's jarring slide. Munson was taped up, and the cut on his chin required three stitches. It didn't go unnoticed by the other Yankee players.

"I don't start any fights," said Jackson. "But I stop a lot of them. If they want to fight, I'll be thrilled. I don't like any of that stuff because it affects my play. Let them do their own thing, and I'll do mine. I don't care if pitchers knock me down a thousand times as long as they don't hit me once."

The Royals were ready to hit New York with their number one Yankee-killer, Paul Splittorff, in the third game. Over the years, the tall left-hander had enjoyed good success against the Yanks. His career record against them was 12–5. He had been scheduled to pitch in the opening game of the series. However, his father had died three days before, and Herzog felt it would have been too much of an emotional strain. So when the series opened in Yankee Stadium, Splittorff was matched against Catfish Hunter.

"I'm right back on schedule," revealed Splittorff. "I pitched batting practice Tuesday and threw ten minutes in the bullpen Wednesday. I've worked up to the game. You try to keep the ball in the alleys, away from the foul lines, just like home."

Lemon had originally scheduled Guidry as his third game starter. But after winning the opener, he reconsidered and switched to Hunter instead.

"We have depended on Guidry so much we may have put too much pressure on him," reasoned Lemon.

The third game was a pressure one, indeed. Whoever won would have an edge with the loser facing instant elimination. The Yankees wanted the edge with Guidry ready to apply the clincher the next day.

George Brett of the Royals hits his third home run of the day in the third playoff game. (Wide World Photos)

Throughout most of the game it was the Yankees against Brett. The pesky third baseman dramatically hit home runs his first three times at bat. No one had ever done that before in the playoffs. Yet, after six innings the Yankees led 4–3, chiefly because Jackson hit a home run and knocked in three runs.

Lemon figured he'd seal the victory by bringing in Gossage for the final three innings. Making his first appearance in the series, Gossage got by the seventh inning without incident, even though Brett flied deep to right-center. However, he ran into trouble in the eighth. The Royals scored twice to take a 5–4 lead and seemed in command.

But Roy White opened the Yankee eighth with a single. Herzog then lifted Splittorff and brought in Doug Bird to face Munson. Though ailing, Munson had a double and single his first three times up. Munson took two balls, then hit a high fastball deep into left-centerfield. It carried into the Kansas City bullpen and gave the Yanks a dramatic 6–5 triumph over the Royals.

"I've never hit one that felt better," said Munson. "I've hit a lot of balls out that way in the last 10 years that have been caught. I didn't think that one would be caught, but I wasn't sure it was high enough to get over the fence.

"I haven't pulled a ball like that in three months. The shoulder has affected my swing more than my throwing. I haven't exactly been too productive, and I never had a season when I've felt this bad. I've had problems since spring training. Ah, why dwell on it? Just because you hit a homer, it doesn't get you well."

Before Munson went up to hit, he talked about Bird with Jackson, who was the next hitter. Nothing really heavy, just waiting for Bird to get ready.

"Thurman just wanted to stay out of the double play and move the runner up," disclosed Jackson. "All he said to me is, 'I hope I don't hit into a double play.' The thing about Thurman is he is always relaxed. He gets ready in a different kind of way than anybody I know. He kind of talks himself down getting himself up.

"I've got the greatest respect for Thurman. He's a great player, and I like him. It's a pleasure playing with him because the man is a genuine pressure player. The man has a sore shoulder, a bum knee, and stitches in his chin and finger. And he goes out and hits the longest ball I've ever seen a right-handed batter hit in Yankee Stadium."

Bucky Dent

Lost in the drama of Munson's homer was Brett's tremendous individual effort. Even when he got up for the last time in the ninth inning, he hit a ball to deep leftfield. He sat sadly, his eyes red from crying.

"I was excited," said Brett. "Of course, I was excited. I've never hit three home runs in my life, not even in batting practice. I'd trade the three home runs for a win. What good did it do for the team? What good did it do for the fans of Kansas City? What good

did it do for my family? I want to play in a World Series, not sit in the stands. I'm not in this just for me."

The Royals were down to their last gasp. The Yanks had Guidry ready for the clincher in the fourth game. Herzog was hoping that Leonard, who had lost the opener, would snap back against the Yankees' best pitcher. The odds were definitely against them.

"They're in rough shape," exclaimed Jackson. "They're down two games to one, and

Thurman Munson rounds third (and Royals' third baseman George Brett) on a two-run homer in the third playoff game. The blast gave the Yanks a 6-5 lead that held up until the end. (World Wide Photos)

now they got to look at Cy Young."

Guidry had performed like a Cy Young Award winner. Easily. He was happy for the extra day's rest.

"If I had a choice, I'd rather pitch on four days' rest," disclosed Guidry. "My arm is a little stiff. I think I need the full four days to come back because I throw so hard. When I'm strong and throwing hard, the hitters aren't going to hit me very much. I don't care if they bring a telephone pole up there.

I'll just go after them the way I've been pitching all year."

And he did. He worked eight innings, gave up one run, yielded seven hits, and struck out seven batters. Gossage took care of the ninth inning to preserve the 2–1 victory that was fashioned by home runs by Nettles in the second and White in the sixth.

It was another Yank comeback. For the third straight game the Royals scored first. A leadoff triple by Brett and a single by Hal

McRae gave the Royals a 1–0 first inning lead. It had Guidry thinking for a moment.

"I stepped back and I said to myself, 'Gee, they hit two good fastballs with something on them,'" revealed Guidry. "I walked behind the mound, took a breath, and said, 'That's all you're gonna get.' That's what I said.

"I had a good fastball. I got by primarily on it. I don't throw that many sliders. I went to it for a couple of innings in the middle of the game, but after that it was fastball, fastball, fastball. If they weren't getting around on my fastball, I knew they weren't gonna get around on Goose's."

They didn't. After Amos Otis led off the ninth inning against Guidry with a double, Gossage got the final three outs that put the Yankees into the World Series.

"I threw nothing but fastballs," said Gossage. "I knew I had good velocity. It's almost automatic for me to throw the fastball in that situation. If I'm going to lose or give up a base hit, it's gonna be on my fastball."

No one felt more contented than White. He was almost a forgotten Yankee who had hardly played in last year's playoffs. This year he won it.

"Last year was a low point," admitted White. "I wasn't a part of what happened last year. Now I'm very happy. I played a role. I've had to prove myself and prove myself over and over again through my whole career, and then I had to prove myself again. The fact that I was able to prove myself this time gives me such tremendous personal satisfaction."

Lemon couldn't have been happier. He was sitting in his office smiling and answering questions.

Royals' action

1978 CHAMPIONSHIP
GAME SUMMARY

GAME 1
at KANSAS CITY
Tuesday, October 3

New York 0 1 1 0 2 0 0 3 0 7 16 0
Kansas City 0 0 0 0 0 1 0 0 0 1 2 2

BEATTIE, Clay (6), and Munson; LEONARD, Mingori (5), Hrabosky (8), Bird (9), and Porter.
HR: New York (1)—Jackson. T—2:57. A—41,143.

GAME 2
at KANSAS CITY
Wednesday, October 4

New York 0 0 0 0 0 0 2 2 0 4 12 1
Kansas City . . . . . . 1 4 0 0 0 0 3 2 x 10 16 1

FIGUEROA, Tidrow (2), Lyle (7), and Munson; GURA, Pattin (7), Hrabosky (8), and Porter.
HR: Kansas City (1)—Patek. T—2:40. A—41,158.

GAME 3
at NEW YORK
Friday, October 6

Kansas City 1 0 1 0 1 0 0 2 0 5 10 1
New York . . . . 0 1 0 2 0 1 0 2 x 6 10 0

Splittorff, BIRD (8), Hrabosky (8), and Porter; Hunter, GOSSAGE (7), and Munson.
HR: Kansas City (3)—Brett; New York (2)—Jackson, Munson. T—2:14. A—55,445.

GAME 4
at NEW YORK
Saturday, October 7

Kansas City 1 0 0 0 0 0 0 0 0 1 7 0
New York . . . . 0 1 0 0 0 1 0 0 x 2 4 0

LEONARD and Porter; GUIDRY, Gossage (9), and Munson.
HR: New York (2)—Nettles, R. White.
T—2:20. A—54,356.

Yankees won — 3 games to 1

STATISTICAL SUMMARY

	NY	OPP		W	L
Errors	1	4	Day	1	1
Double Play	2	4	Night	2	0
Comp Games	0	1	Sho-Indv	0	0
Stolen Base	0	6	Sho-Team	0	0
Caught Stlg	1	3	1-Run Gm	2	0
Doubles	3	6	2-Run Gm	0	0
Triples	1	3	Extra Inn	0	0
Homers-Home	4	3	VS Right	3	0
Homers-Road	1	1	VS Left	0	1
Homers-Tot	5	4	Dbl-Hdr	0	0
LF on Base	27	23	Split	0	
			Starters	2	1
			Relief	1	0
			Streaks	2*	1

ATTENDANCE

	HOME	ROAD
Total	111801	82328
Ave.	55901	41164
Dates	2	2
Games	2	2

AMERICAN LEAGUE CHAMPIONSHIP SERIES — 1978

KANSAS CITY ROYALS

Batter	PCT	G	AB	R	H	2B	3B	HR	RBI	BB	SO	SH	SF	HP	SB	CS	E
Braun	.000	2	5	0	0	0	0	0	0	1	1	0	0	0	0	0	0
Brett	.389	4	18	7	7	1	1	3	3	0	1	0	0	0	0	0	1
Cowens	.133	4	15	2	2	0	0	0	1	0	2	0	0	0	0	0	0
Hurdle	.375	4	8	1	3	0	1	0	1	2	3	0	0	0	0	0	0
LaCock	.364	4	11	1	4	2	1	0	1	3	1	0	0	0	1	0	0
McRae	.214	4	14	0	3	0	0	0	2	2	2	1	1	0	1	1	0
Otis	.429	4	14	2	6	2	0	0	1	3	5	0	0	0	4	0	1
Patek	.077	4	13	2	1	0	0	1	2	1	4	0	0	0	0	1	2
Poquette	.000	1	1	0	0	0	0	0	0	0	0	0	0	0	0	0	0
Porter	.357	4	14	1	5	1	0	0	3	2	0	0	1	0	0	0	0
Wathan	.000	1	3	0	0	0	0	0	0	0	0	0	0	0	0	0	0
White	.231	4	13	1	3	0	0	0	2	0	0	0	0	0	0	0	0
Wilson L	.000		0	0	0	0	0	0	0	0	0	0	0	0	0	0	0
Wilson .....R	.250		4	0	1	0	0	0	0	0	2	0	0	0	0	1	0
Wilson ......T	.250	3	4	0	1	0	0	0	0	0	2	0	0	0	0	1	0
DH Hitters	.214		14	0	3	0	0	0	2	2	2	1	1	0	1	1	0
PH Hitters	.000		4	0	0	0	0	0	0	1	2	0	0	0	0	0	0
TOTALS	.263		133	17	35	6	3	4	16	14	21	1	2	0	6	3	4

Pitcher	ERA	W	L	AP	GS	CG	SV	SHO	IP	H	R	ER	HR	BB	SO	HB	WP
Bird	9.00	0	1	2	0	0	0	0	1.0	2	1	1	1	0	1	0	0
Gura	2.84	1	0	1	1	0	0	0	6.1	8	2	2	0	2	2	0	0
Hrabosky	3.00	0	0	3	0	0	0	0	3.0	3	1	1	1	0	2	0	0
Leonard	3.75	0	2	2	2	1	0	0	12.0	13	5	5	2	2	11	0	1
Mingori	7.36	0	0	1	0	0	0	0	3.2	5	3	3	0	3	0	0	0
Pattin	27.00	0	0	1	0	0	0	0	0.2	2	2	2	0	0	0	0	0
Splittorff	4.91	0	0	1	1	0	0	0	7.1	9	5	4	1	0	2	0	0
TOTALS	4.76	1	3	11	4	1	0	0	34.0	42	19	18	5	7	18	0	1

NEW YORK YANKEES

Batter	PCT	G	AB	R	H	2B	3B	HR	RBI	BB	SO	SH	SF	HP	SB	CS	E
Blair	.000	4	6	1	0	0	0	0	0	0	1	0	0	0	0	0	0
Chambliss	.400	4	15	1	6	0	0	0	2	0	4	0	0	0	0	0	0
Dent	.200	4	15	0	3	0	0	0	4	0	0	0	0	0	0	0	1
Doyle	.236	3	7	0	2	0	0	0	1	1	1	0	0	0	0	0	0
Jackson	.462	4	13	5	6	1	0	2	6	3	4	0	1	0	0	1	0
Johnson	.000	1	1	0	0	0	0	0	0	0	0	0	0	0	0	0	0
Munson	.278	4	18	2	5	1	0	1	2	0	0	0	0	0	0	0	0
Nettles	.333	4	15	3	5	0	1	1	2	0	1	0	0	0	0	0	0
Piniella	.235	4	17	2	4	0	0	0	0	0	3	0	0	0	0	0	0
Rivers	.455	4	11	0	5	0	0	0	0	2	0	0	0	0	0	0	0
Stanley	.200	2	5	0	1	0	0	0	0	0	2	0	0	0	0	0	0
Thomasson	.000	3	1	0	0	0	0	0	0	0	0	0	0	0	0	0	0
White L	.286		7	2	2	1	0	1	1	0	1	0	0	0	0	0	0
White ......R	.333		9	3	3	0	0	0	0	1	1	0	0	0	0	0	0
White ....T	.313	4	16	5	5	1	0	1	1	1	2	0	0	0	0	0	0
DH Hitters	.462		13	5	6	1	0	2	6	2	4	0	1	0	0	1	0
PH Hitters	.000		4	0	0	0	0	0	0	0	0	0	0	0	0	0	0
TOTALS	.300		140	19	42	3	1	5	18	7	18	0	1	0	0	1	1

Pitcher	ERA	W	L	AP	GS	CG	SV	SHO	IP	H	R	ER	HR	BB	SO	HB	WP
Beattie	1.69	1	0	1	1	0	0	0	5.1	2	1	1	0	5	3	0	0
Clay	.00	0	0	1	0	0	1	0	3.2	0	0	0	0	3	2	0	0
Figueroa	27.00	0	1	1	1	0	0	0	1.0	5	5	3	0	0	0	0	0
Gossage	4.50	1	0	2	0	0	1	0	4.0	3	2	2	0	0	3	0	0
Guidry	1.12	1	0	1	1	0	0	0	8.0	7	1	1	0	1	7	0	0
Hunter	4.50	0	0	1	1	0	0	0	6.0	7	3	3	3	3	5	0	0
Lyle	13.50	0	0	1	0	0	0	0	1.1	3	2	2	0	0	0	0	0
Tidrow	4.76	0	0	1	0	0	0	0	5.2	8	3	3	1	2	1	0	0
TOTALS	3.86	3	1	9	4	0	2	0	35.0	35	17	15	4	14	21	0	0

AMERICAN LEAGUE CHAMPIONSHIP SERIES
Game One

New York	AB	R	H	BI	Kansas City	AB	R	H	BI
Rivers, CF	5	0	2	0	Braun, LF	4	0	0	0
Blair, CF	1	1	0	0	Brett, 3B	4	1	1	0
Munson, C	5	0	1	0	Otis, CF	2	0	0	0
Piniella, RF	5	2	2	0	Porter, C	3	0	0	0
Jackson, DH	3	2	3	3	LaCock, 1B	2	0	0	0
Nettles, 3B	5	1	2	1	McRae, DH	2	0	0	1
Chamblss, 1B	5	0	2	1	Cowens, RF	4	0	1	0
R White, LF	4	1	1	0	Patek, SS	3	0	0	0
Doyle, 2B	5	0	2	1	Hurdle, PH	0	0	0	0
Dent, SS	5	0	1	1	F White, 2B	3	0	0	0
Total	43	7	16	7	Poquette, PH	1	0	0	0
					Total	28	1	2	1

```
New York          011    020    030—7
Kansas City       000    001    000—1
```

E—Otis, Brett. LOB—New York 12, Kansas City 9. 2B—R White, Jackson, Brett. 3B—Nettles. HR—Jackson. SB—Otis, LaCock. SF—McRae.

	IP	H	R	ER	BB	SO
New York						
Beattie W	5½	2	1	1	5	3
Clay	3⅓	0	0	0	3	2
Kansas City						
Leonard L	4	9	3	3	0	2
Mingori	3⅔	5	3	3	3	0
Hrabosky	⅓	1	1	1	0	0
Bird	1	1	0	0	0	1

Save—Clay. PB—Porter. T—2:57. A—41,143.

Game Two

New York	AB	R	H	BI		Kansas City	AB	R	H	BI
Rivers CF	3	0	2	0		Brett 3B	5	2	2	0
Thomasn CF	1	0	0	0		McRae DH	3	0	2	0
Munson C	5	0	0	0		Otis CF	5	1	3	1
Piniella LF	5	0	0	0		Porter C	4	0	2	2
Jackson RF	4	1	1	0		LaCock 1B	5	1	2	1
Nettles 3B	4	1	1	0		Hurdle LF	3	1	2	1
Chambliss 1B	4	1	4	1		Wilson LF	1	0	0	0
R White DH	4	1	1	0		Cowens RF	4	2	1	0
Stanley 2B	2	0	1	0		Patek SS	4	2	1	2
Johnson PH	1	0	0	0		F White 2B	4	1	1	2
Doyle 2B	0	0	0	0						
Blair 2B	1	0	0	0						
Dent SS	4	0	2	3						
Total	38	4	12	4		Total	38	10	16	9

```
New York        000   000   220—4
Kansas City     140   000   32x—10
```

E—Patek, Dent. DP—Kansas City 2, LOB—New York 9, Kansas City 8. 2B—La-Cock. 3B—Hurdle. HR—Patek (1). SB—Otis 2, S—McRae. SF—Porter.

	IP	H	R	ER	BB	SO
New York						
Figueroa L	1	5	5	3	0	0
Tidrow	5⅔	8	3	3	2	1
Lyle	1⅓	3	2	2	0	0
Kansas City						
Gura W	6⅓	8	2	2	2	2
Pattin	⅔	2	2	2	0	0
Hrabosky	2	2	0	0	0	1

Figueroa faced 4 batters in 2nd; Pattin faced 2 batters in 7th.
T—2:40. A—41,158.

Game Three

Kansas City	AB	R	H	BI		New York	AB	R	H	BI
Brett 3B	5	3	3	3		Rivers CF	1	0	1	0
McRae DH	5	0	0	0		Blair CF	3	0	0	0
Otis CF	3	1	2	0		R White LF	4	2	2	0
Porter C	4	1	2	1		Thomasn LF	0	0	0	0
LaCock 1B	3	0	2	0		Munson C	4	2	3	2
Hurdle LF	4	0	1	0		Jackson DH	3	2	2	3
Wilson LF	0	0	0	0		Piniella RF	4	0	2	0
Cowens RF	4	0	0	1		Nettles 3B	3	0	0	0
Patek SS	3	0	0	0		Chambliss 1b	3	0	0	0
F White 2B	3	0	0	0		Stanley 2B	3	0	0	0
Braun PH	1	0	0	0		Dent SS	3	0	0	0
Total	35	5	10	5		Total	31	6	10	5

```
Kansas City     101   010   020—5
New York        010   201   02x—6
```

E—Patek. DP—Kansas City 2, New York
LOB—Kansas City & New York 2, 2B—LaCock. Porter, Munson, Otis. 3B—La-Cock. HR—Brett 3, Jackson, Munson. SB—Otis SF—Jackson.

	IP	H	R	ER	BB	SO
Kansas City						
Splittorff	7 1/3	9	5	4	0	2
Bird (L)	0	1	1	1	0	0
Hrabosky	2/3	0	0	0	0	1
New York						
Hunter	6	7	3	3	3	5
Gossage (W)	3	3	2	2	0	2

Bird faced one batter in 8th
PB—Munson. T—2:14. A—55,445.

Game Four

New York	AB	R	H	BI	Kansas City	AB	R	H	BI
Rivers CF	2	0	0	0	Brett 3B	4	1	1	0
Blair CF	1	0	0	0	McRae DH	4	0	1	1
R White LF	4	1	1	1	Otis CF	4	0	1	0
Thomasn LF	0	0	0	0	Cowens RF	3	0	0	0
Munson C	4	0	1	0	Hurdle PH	1	0	0	0
Jackson DH	3	0	0	0	Porter C	3	0	1	0
Piniella RF	3	0	0	0	Wathan 1B	3	0	0	0
Nettles 3B	3	1	2	1	LaCock PH	1	0	0	0
Chambliss 1B	3	0	0	0	F White 2B	3	0	2	0
Doyle 2B	2	0	0	0	Patek SS	3	0	0	0
Dent SS	3	0	0	0	Wilson LF	3	0	1	0
Total	28	2	4	2	Total	32	1	7	1

Kansas City	100	000	000—1
New York	010	001	00x—2

DP—New York 1. LOB—Kansas City 5, New York 4. 2B—Otis. 3B—Brett. HR—Nettles, R White. SB—McRae.

	IP	H	R	ER	BB	SO
Kansas City						
Leonard (L)	8	4	2	2	2	9
New York						
Guidry (W)	8	7	1	1	1	7
Gossage	1	0	0	0	0	1

Guidry faced one batter in 9th
Save—Gossage. WP—Leonard. T—2:20. A—56,356.

"The best damn club I've ever been given the opportunity to play, I mean watch," smiled Lemon. "Good players make you smart, don't they? Being replaced like I was in Chicago and now finding out I'm smart as hell. I was prepared to loaf all summer, and believe me, I do that better than anybody.

"When you're playing you can do certain things. When you're a manager you have to suffer, and these guys sure made an old man out of me."

"Was destiny behind the Yankee win?" someone asked.

"Make it dynasty," answered Al Rosen, "not destiny. The Yankees have always been a dynasty, haven't they?"

"A dynasty doesn't fall 14 games behind," pointed out Lemon. "Let's call it a dynasty-destiny. I still can't describe my feelings. This has been my most gratifying year in baseball. Give me another day to enjoy what happened; then I'll start worrying about the Dodgers."

They were next . . .

Brian Doyle

10

World Series

There was laughter. Everyone was celebrating. The Yankee players had devoured the cases of champagne that were the hallmark of winning the American League pennant. But some of the players wanted to celebrate into the night. And why not? They had staged the biggest comeback in the history of the American League amid chaos and turmoil of their own doing. Just when the experts had written them off, they miraculously overcame their vindictiveness and won their third straight pennant. They were truly the damn Yankees to others in the league.

Reggie Jackson was the happiest of all. He had been a main character in the three penny opera that was the Yankees. But in the laughter of the clubhouse, nobody remembered the dissonant chords of the season-long aria. Now was the moment for merriment. The Dodgers and the World Series were 72 hours away. Jackson, for one, wanted to party some more, along the upper

East Side where the young people congregate.

"I got the tab, Thurman," yelled Jackson. "And if I don't pick it up, you can pick it up. And if you don't pick it up, George can pick it up.

"He fouled you up 80 times; and he fouled me up, too. I know we agree on that. I'll get the tab or you will; and if we don't, George will; and if he doesn't, we'll slap the hell out of him."

Munson smiled. So did Jackson. Steinbrenner was the butt of the humor. Munson and Jackson were smiling, together, talking about going out with one another. It was the happiest the Yankee clubhouse had been all season long. Then Jackson got serious for a moment.

"There's respect on both sides," said Jackson. "Warmth? You can't play with a guy like Munson and not like him; and if you don't like him, you still have to respect him. I think

Lou Piniella

he likes me, yes. And on top of everything, he's a great player."

The World Series was designed to open in Los Angeles on Tuesday night. The first two games of the October classic were to be played there. The next three were scheduled for Yankee Stadium. And if any more games were needed in the best-of-seven challenge, the combatants would return to Los Angeles for the final two contests.

Once more the Yankees were established as underdogs. The Las Vegas bet parlors favored the Dodgers in the opening game and for the remainder of the Series. Apparently, the smart money set doesn't believe in miracles.

"When you've come back from so far behind, it'd seem a waste if we don't win the whole thing," said Roy White. "We're getting into something that not too many people

have done, winning the World Series twice in a row. We're the defending world champions, and we're not even the favorite. But I guess when you come right down to it, we've been the underdog a lot this year."

Despite his failure in post-season play, Ed Figueroa was nevertheless picked by Lemon to oppose Tommy John and the Dodgers. There was a certain pall in the Dodger clubhouse. Just 48 hours before, their popular coach, Jim Gilliam, who had been with the organization for 26 years, died of heart failure after suffering a stroke three weeks earlier. The Dodgers dedicated the Series to Gilliam, each wearing a round, black patch with the number 19 in white on his left sleeve. They were carrying his memory into battle.

"There is no doubt in my mind that we're going to win this thing," said Dodger captain

Davey Lopes. "Jimmy's spirit is in each of our players. They will have to beat 50 of us, not just 25. We have something to do, not just for the fans or ourselves, but for Junior; and I really believe that will give us the edge."

The game was also a big one for Figueroa. He was hearing the whispers that he could never win the meaningful games. He was aware of his past performance.

"This means a lot to me because I haven't won games for these guys the last two years in the playoffs and Series," lamented Figueroa. "I help them get here, but I don't win one. The Dodgers hit the ball good like Boston, and I concentrate better against a good hitting team. And at least they haven't seen my curveball and the way I pitch."

The Dodgers didn't have to see much of Figueroa in the opening game. They chased him with a three-run outbreak in the second inning and easily went on to trounce the Yankees, 11–5. It was Lopes who smacked a two-run homer off a hanging curveball that spelled Figueroa's doom. The solemn Dodger captain went on to hit another, finishing the night with five runs batted in. Figueroa lost his fourth straight championship game in the last three years, saddled with a 7.86 ERA.

Figueroa couldn't explain his failure. Something had to be wrong.

"I was really looking forward to this game because I haven't won one yet," moaned Figueroa. "I know I'm a better pitcher than I was tonight. Maybe I'm trying too hard."

Whatever, the Yankees needed better pitching to win. Lou Piniella admitted it.

"What did I say yesterday?" asked Piniella. "If we don't get good pitching, there's no way we can win. We've got to get good pitching to win. We've got to."

Lemon hoped to get such from Catfish Hunter in the second game. Hunter finished strong in the second half of the Yanks' miracle season and was a veteran of October play. His mound rival was Burt Hooton who, like Hunter, finished strong, winning 14 of his last 18 decisions.

"These last two days we've been thinking too much," offered Hunter. "And when you start thinking, that's when you get in trouble."

Hunter didn't get into trouble until the sixth inning. He made a bad pitch to Ron Cey, and the Dodger third baseman cracked a three-run homer. The blow wiped out a 2–1 lead and eventually gave the Dodgers their second straight win, 4–3, with Cey knocking in all four runs.

The Series had its most dramatic moment with two out in the ninth inning. The Yanks had runners on first and second and Jackson at bat. The powerful slugger had accounted for all of his team's runs with a two-run homer and a grounder. Opposing Jackson was 21-year-old Bob Welch, a flame-throwing righty who had been with the Dodgers only since mid-season.

It was a classic confrontation, power against power. Jackson swung at the first fastball and missed. The crowd roared. Then Welch delivered a hummer in tight that brushed Jackson back. The next three pitches that Welch fired were fouled off. Then Welch threw high to even the count at 2–2. Jackson fouled the next pitch. The tension mounted when Welch's next offering was

Ron Guidry delivers first pitch of third game of the World Series to Davey Lopes of the Dodgers. Lopes flied out. (Wide World Photos)

outside. The count was now full. The crowd was excited. Jackson fixed his glasses. He stepped back to hit. He was ready. So was Welch. He fired a fastball high and inside. Jackson cut and missed as the crowd went wild.

"The guy beat me," said Jackson. "Too big a swing. He threw the ball by me. I didn't see anything but fastballs. Aviation fuel all the way. High octane. The kid came right at me. Beat me fair and square."

It was Welch's biggest thrill in his young career. He felt the drama.

"The adrenalin was flowing," disclosed Welch. "He stepped out a couple of times, and that built up things some more. Two out, 3–2, Reggie Jackson. It's something I'll never forget. No one will."

That said it all. No one had to say that the Yanks were in trouble. They were down, 2–0, and no team in the 74-year history of the World Series had ever come back from that kind of deficit to emerge victorious. The Yanks had their backs to the wall, even though they were back in Yankee Stadium for the next three games. Whenever they were in trouble during the season, they turned to Ron Guidry. He was expected to stop the skid against Don Sutton.

"I don't feel there is any more pressure on me than usual," revealed Guidry. "I've learned to live with it. They have tremendous talent, but I'm a power pitcher, and it will be my power versus their power. I just hope to have a little extra to get by."

What Guidry had was Graig Nettles. Without his unbelievable play at third base the Yanks might not have had a 5–1 victory. It was just that Guidry wasn't as sharp as he normally was, walking seven, striking out only four, and surrendering eight hits.

Psychologically, Nettles destroyed the Dodgers. He was so good that Lemon quipped afterwards, "Nettles should get the save. In 41 years I've seen a lot of plays, but I don't think anybody has played third base better than that."

Nettles' brilliant performance with his magic glove foiled six Dodger rallies. Not budding rallies, but ones in which a base hit would have led to runs that clearly would have erased a 2–1 Yank lead. He leaped, dove, and speared balls that seemingly were base hits in the second inning, twice in the third, twice more in the fifth, and again in the sixth. When Lopes came to bat in the ninth inning, he motioned for Nettles to come away from third base.

"I took it as a compliment," smiled Nettles.

Other Dodgers were complimentary.

"If we weren't losing, I would have stood up and applauded, myself," remarked Reggie Smith. "How could anyone be better? I've never seen a display like that. All he did was the impossible, play after play."

Lopes agreed.

"It was the greatest exhibition I've ever seen," he acknowledged. "It's frustrating that Nettles made about six great plays. You expect him to make one great play, but he made six."

It was all perfectly natural to Nettles. There's really no way to explain it.

"They're reaction plays," said Nettles. "You don't have time to think, just react. I can't explain them. I react and let my instincts and coordination take over."

Lemon was confident that Figueroa would finally take over. He named him to pitch in the fourth game and even the Series at two games each. As in the opener, Figueroa was opposing John.

"It's like going to a dance," explained Lemon. "I go home with the guy who brought me. Using Figgy was in the back of my mind all the time. I can't see how you can pass up a 20-game winner."

This time Figueroa lasted five innings. When he was removed, the Yanks were behind, 3–0, on Smith's three-run homer. John looked in command. However, a controversial play in the sixth inning led to two runs and got the Yanks back in the contest.

With White on second and Munson on first, Jackson drove in the Yanks' first run with a single to rightfield. Piniella hit a line drive to the left of Bill Russell. The Dodger shortstop stretched and caught the ball and then dropped it. He quickly picked up the ball, stepped on second base, and threw to first in an attempt to double up Jackson and end the inning. The ball hit Jackson on his right thigh and rolled past first baseman Steve Garvey. Munson scored from second base; Jackson was called out, and Piniella was ruled safe at first. The Dodgers argued that Jackson made no attempt to avoid Russell's throw, that he deliberately let himself be hit to avoid the double play.

The play was important. The Yankees went on to tie the game in the eighth and then won it in the tenth inning 4–3 when White walked, Jackson singled, and Piniella clubbed a high fastball to right-center off Welch for a game-winning single. The Yanks had succeeded in evening the Series at 2–2.

"He throws fastballs, nothing but fastballs," exclaimed Piniella. "Very fast balls. I believe it's easier to gear yourself up when you know what's coming. It was a bad pitch, too high. I could've popped it up or hit a fly ball on it, too."

Russell was upset by the umpire's call that averted the double play.

"Reggie saw the ball coming," said Russell. "He moved right into it. That's interference."

Russell was more upset the next day. He not only made an error in the Yanks' lopsided 12–2 victory, but he was the subject of some questionable play around shortstop as well. Jim Beattie, a rookie pitching his first complete major league game, beat Hooton, a veteran, as the Yankees set a World Series record by hitting 18 singles. Munson led the way with three of them and knocked in five runs.

"Look, I'm not making any excuses," began Russell. "I missed the first one; but those others, gosh, they'd have been tough outs. I'm only human. I'm not a golden glove, by any means."

Beattie was as happy as Russell was sad. It was the biggest win of his young career. The victory now gave the Yanks a 3–2 edge.

"This is something I've been looking forward to all year," beamed Beattie. "How I feel is hard to describe. I didn't think I'd be here at the end of the year from where I was in the middle of the year. Clyde King worked

on fundamentals with me, but Billy Martin was the one who suggested the no-windup."

It was also suggested that the Dodgers were coming apart. They seemed to come unglued in the 12–2 carnage. The only solace they found was in the return to Los Angeles. They were going home, but the Yankees weren't at all concerned. They were the ones with the edge now.

"I think we've got it," expressed Bucky Dent, who had been quietly having a good Series along with Brian Doyle, each hitting well over .300. "Guidry turned it around Friday night along with Nettles' great defensive plays. Our confidence is very high right now. We beat Boston in Boston, and we can beat Los Angeles in Los Angeles.

"We've been under pressure for so long that it seems like this team plays better under pressure, plays harder. What amazes me is that we've got guys hurt, and they still won't quit. They don't ever want to quit."

The telling sign for the Dodgers was that they left New York complaining. They found fault with the infield, the fans, and the New York writers. What they should have been concerned with was why Steve Garvey, Reggie Smith, Dusty Baker, and Rick Monday weren't hitting. Manager Tom Lasorda sent Sutton out to the mound to battle Hunter and stop their three-game skid.

It was close for three innings, with the Yanks ahead, 3–2. But the Yankees weren't going to be denied the championship they had fought so hard for all year. They scored two runs in the sixth, and then Jackson put it away for good with a two-run homer in the seventh for a 7–2 victory. The Yankees had won a second straight world championship. It was Hunter's first World Series win in three years. Yet, quietly, Doyle and Dent, the last two batters in the lineup, did the most damage. Each had three hits as Dent knocked in three runs and Doyle two.

Dent was named the Series' most valuable player. He batted .417, 10 for 24, leading the Yanks in hits and tied in runs batted in with eight. Doyle made his presence felt by going 7 for 16, a .438 average.

Graig Nettles hustles to stop grounder off bat of Dodgers' Steve Garvey in the third game. Nettles then threw to second to force out Reggie Smith. (Wide World Photos)

Joe Ferguson

The Yankees really turned it on in the clubhouse. They defied all odds in coming back from the opening two losses to sweep the next four games. Indeed, they had won their second straight championship in dramatic style.

"We've got some big hearts on this team," exclaimed Dent. "People say we're the best team money can buy, but you don't buy hearts; you don't buy what's inside of them. I think this is the best thing that ever happened to baseball. What we've done will give a lot of teams years from now incentive.

They'll say, 'Hey, look at the '78 Yankees. They didn't quit.'"

Hunter, for one, didn't. Twice he came off the disabled list ultimately to become a factor in the Yankees' pennant push.

"This win means as much to me as any I've ever won," said Hunter. "I enjoyed this one more than anything else. To have contributed to a team that came back like this, all year. This is the greatest team I ever played on. I can't believe we won it all. It seems like a dream."

It was a dream that Billy Martin began,

In the fifth game, Garvey got a single, as Graig Nettles went up in the air to stop the ball. (Wide World Photos)

about being a Yankee and winning. Piniella remembered it.

"Billy Martin showed this team how to be champions," emphasized Piniella without taking anything away from Lemon. "He came to the Yankees when we had never won a thing, and he showed us how to win.

"When Billy took over in 1975, we had a lot of guys who had never played on a winner, except for Catfish Hunter. Billy told us that we should be winning. He always had confidence in us, and now we have it in ourselves. If Billy Martin had never been Yankee man-

ager, we might have never started winning."

That's what it's all about. Besides Martin, nobody likes winning more than Steinbrenner. On the happy plane that carried the Yankees back, he conferred with Gene Monahan, the team's trainer. He wanted Monahan to scout the colleges, looking for new talent.

"I'm getting ready for next year," snapped Steinbrenner.

It should be interesting again, but perhaps not as interesting as 1980 . . .

1978 WORLD SERIES
GAME SUMMARIES

GAME 1
at LOS ANGELES
Tuesday, October 10

New York 0 0 0 0 0 0 3 2 0 5 9 1
Los Angeles ......0 3 0 3 1 0 3 1 x 11 15 2
FIGUEROA, Clay (2), Lindblad (5), Tidrow (7), and Munson; JOHN, Forster (8), and Yeager.
HR: New York (1)—Jackson; Los Angeles (3)—Baker, Lopes (2). T—2:48. A—55,997.

GAME 4
at NEW YORK
Saturday, October 14

Los Angeles ...0 0 0 0 3 0 0 0 0 0 3 6 1
New York 0 0 0 0 0 2 0 1 0 1 4 9 0
John, Forster (8), WELCH (8), Yeager, and Grote; Figueroa, Tidrow (6), GOSSAGE (9), and Munson.
HR: Los Angeles (1)—Smith. T—3:17. A—56,445.

GAME 2
at LOS ANGELES
Wednesday, October 11

New York 0 0 2 0 0 0 1 0 0 3 11 0
Los Angeles ......0 0 0 1 0 3 0 0 x 4 7 0
HUNTER, Gossage (7), and Munson; HOOTON, Forster (7), Welch (9), and Yeager.
HR: Los Angeles (1)—Coy. T—2:38. A—55,982.

GAME 5
at NEW YORK
Sunday, October 15

Los Angeles 1 0 1 0 0 0 0 0 0 2 9 3
New York ....0 0 4 3 0 0 4 1 x 12 18 0
HOOTON, Rautzhan (3), Hough (4), Yeager, and Oates; BEATTIE and Munson, Heath.
HR: none. T—2:56. A—65,448.

GAME 3
at NEW YORK
Friday, October 13

Los Angeles 0 0 1 0 0 0 0 0 0 1 8 0
New York ....1 1 0 0 0 0 3 0 x 5 10 1
SUTTON, Rautzhan (7), Hough (8), Yeager, and Grote; GUIDRY and Munson.
HR: New York (1)—White. T—2:27. A—56,447.

GAME 6
at LOS ANGELES
Tuesday, October 17

New York 0 3 0 0 2 2 0 0 7 11 0
Los Angeles 1 0 1 0 0 0 0 0 0 2 7 1
HUNTER, Gossage (8), and Munson; SUTTON, Welch (6), Rau (8), and Ferguson.
HR: New York (1)—Jackson; Los Angeles (1)—Lopes. T—2:34. A—55,985.

Yankees won—4 games to 2

1978 WORLD SERIES

LOS ANGELES DODGERS

Batter	AVG	G	AB	R	H	2B	3B	HR	RBI	TBB	IBB	SO	SB	CS	PO	A	E	PCT.
Baker	.238	6	21	2	5	0	0	1	1	1	0	3	0	0	12	0	0	1.000
Cey	.286	6	21	2	6	0	0	1	4	3	0	3	0	0	2	12	0	1.000
Davalillo	.333	2	3	0	1	0	0	0	0	0	0	0	0	0	0	0	0	.000
Ferguson	.500	2	4	1	2	2	0	0	0	0	0	1	0	0	11	0	1	.917
Garvey	.208	6	24	1	5	1	0	0	0	1	0	7	1	0	58	3	1	.984
Grote	.000	2	0	0	0	0	0	0	0	0	0	0	0	0	3	0	0	1.000
Lacy	.143	4	14	0	2	0	0	0	1	1	0	3	0	0	0	0	0	.000
Lopes	.308	6	26	7	8	0	0	3	7	2	0	1	3	0	10	19	1	.967
Martinez									Did not play									
Monday	.154	5	13	2	2	1	0	0	0	4	0	3	0	1	5	0	0	1.000
Mota	.000	1	0	0	0	0	0	0	0	1	0	0	0	0	0	0	0	.000
North	.125	4	8	2	1	1	0	0	2	1	0	0	1	0	7	0	0	1.000
Oates	1.000	1	1	0	1	0	0	0	0	1	0	0	0	0	3	1	0	1.000
Russell	.423	6	26	1	11	2	0	0	2	2	0	2	1	2	11	20	3	.912
Smith	.200	6	25	3	5	0	0	1	5	2	0	6	0	1	11	1	1	.923
Yeager	.231	5	13	2	3	1	0	0	0	1	0	2	0	0	23	2	0	1.000
Forster	.000	3	0	0	0	0	0	0	0	0	0	0	0	0	0	1	0	1.000
Hooton	.000	2	0	0	0	0	0	0	0	0	0	0	0	0	1	0	0	1.000
Hough	.000	2	0	0	0	0	0	0	0	0	0	0	0	0	1	0	0	1.000
John	.000	2	0	0	0	0	0	0	0	0	0	0	0	0	0	4	0	1.000
Rau	.000	1	0	0	0	0	0	0	0	0	0	0	0	0	0	1	0	1.000
Rautzhan	.000	2	0	0	0	0	0	0	0	0	0	0	0	0	0	0	0	.000
Sutton	.000	2	0	0	0	0	0	0	0	0	0	0	0	0	0	0	0	.000
Welch	.000	3	0	0	0	0	0	0	0	0	0	0	0	0	0	0	0	.000
TOTALS	.231	6	199	23	52	8	0	6	22	20	0	31	5	4	158	64	7	.969

Passed Balls — Yeager, Oates

Pitcher	ERA	W	L	G	GS	CG	SV	IP	H	R	ER	HR	TBB	IBB	SO	HP
Forster	0.00	0	0	3	0	0	0	4.0	5	0	0	0	1	0	6	1
Hooton	6.48	1	1	2	2	0	0	8.1	13	7	6	0	3	1	6	1
Hough	8.43	0	0	2	0	0	0	5.1	10	5	5	0	2	0	5	0
John	3.07	1	0	2	2	0	0	14.2	14	8	5	1	4	0	6	0
Rau	0.00	0	0	1	0	0	0	2.0	1	0	0	0	0	0	3	0
Rautzhan	13.50	0	0	2	0	0	0	2.0	4	3	3	0	0	0	0	0
Rhoden								Did not pitch								
Sutton	7.50	0	2	2	2	0	0	12.0	17	10	10	1	4	0	8	0
Welch	6.23	0	1	3	0	0	1	4.1	4	3	3	1	2	0	6	0
TOTALS	5.47	2	4	6	6	0	1	52.2	68	36	32	3	16	1	40	2

Wild Pitches — Hooton, Hough, Sutton

NEW YORK YANKEES

Batter	AVG	G	AB	R	H	2B	3B	HR	RBI	TBB	IBB	SO	SB	CS	PO	A	E	PCT.
Blair	.375	6	8	2	3	1	0	0	0	1	0	4	0	0	5	0	0	1.000
Chambliss	.182	3	11	1	2	0	0	0	0	1	0	1	0	0	18	0	0	1.000
Dent	.417	6	24	3	10	1	0	0	7	1	0	2	0	0	8	16	2	.923
Doyle	.438	6	16	4	7	1	0	0	2	0	0	0	0	0	16	7	0	1.000
Heath	.000	1	0	0	0	0	0	0	0	0	0	0	0	0	0	0	0	.000
Jackson	.391	6	23	2	9	1	0	2	8	3	1	7	0	0	0	0	0	.000
Johnson	.000	2	2	0	0	0	0	0	0	0	0	1	0	0	0	0	0	.000
Johnstone	.000	2	0	0	0	0	0	0	0	0	0	0	0	0	1	0	0	1.000
Munson	.329	6	25	5	8	3	0	0	7	3	0	7	1	0	33	5	0	1.000
Nettles	.169	6	25	2	4	0	0	0	1	0	0	6	0	0	8	18	0	1.000
Piniella	.280	6	25	3	7	0	0	0	4	0	0	0	1	0	14	1	0	1.000
Rivers	.333	5	18	2	6	0	0	0	1	0	0	2	1	1	7	0	0	1.000
Spencer	.167	4	12	3	2	0	0	0	0	2	0	4	0	0	23	2	0	1.000
Stanley	.200	3	5	0		1	0	0	0	1	0	0	0	0	5	2	0	1.000
Thomasson	.260	3	4	0	1	0	0	0	0	0	0	1	0	1	3	0	0	1.000
White	.333	6	24	9	8	0	0	1	4	4	0	5	2	0	15	0	0	1.000
DH*	.391	6	23	2	9	1	0	2	8	3	1	7	0	0	0	0	0	.000
Beattie	.000	1	0	0	0	0	0	0	0	0	0	0	0	0	0	1	0	1.000
Clay	.000	1	0	0	0	0	0	0	0	0	0	0	0	0	0	0	0	.000
Figueroa	.000	2	0	0	0	0	0	0	0	0	0	0	0	0	0	0	0	.000
Gossage	.000	3	0	0	0	0	0	0	0	0	0	0	0	0	0	0	0	.000
Guidry	.000	1	0	0	0	0	0	0	0	0	0	0	0	0	1	1	0	1.000
Hunter	.000	2	0	0	0	0	0	0	0	0	0	0	0	0	2	0	0	1.000
Lindblad	.000	1	0	0	0	0	0	0	0	0	0	0	0	0	0	0	0	.000
Tidrow	.000	2	0	0	0	0	0	0	0	0	0	0	0	0	0	0	0	.000
TOTALS	.306	6	222	36	68	8	0	3	34	16	1	40	5	2	159	53	2	.991

*Jackson only DH   SH-White   HBP-Jackson (2)

Pitcher	ERA	W	L	G	GS	CG	SV	IP	H	R	ER	HR	TBB	IBB	SO	HP
Beattie	2.00	1	0	1	1	1	0	9.0	9	2	2	0	4	0	8	0
Clay	11.57	0	0	1	0	0	0	2.1	4	4	3	1	2	0	2	0
Figueroa	8.10	0	1	2	2	0	0	6.2	9	6	6	3	5	0	2	0
Gossage	0.00	1	0	3	0	0	0	6.0	1	0	0	0	1	0	4	0
Guidry	1.00	1	0	1	1	1	0	9.0	8	1	1	0	7	0	4	0
Hunter	4.15	1	1	2	2	0	0	13.0	13	6	6	2	1	0	5	0
Lindblad	11.57	0	0	1	0	0	0	2.1	4	3	3	0	0	0	1	0
Lyle	. . . . Did not pitch															
Tidrow	1.93	0	0	2	0	0	0	4.2	4	1	1	0	0	0	5	0
TOTALS	3.74	4	2	6	6	2	0	53.0	52	23	22	6	20	0	31	0

Wild Pitch-Clay

SERIES COMPOSITE BOX SCORE FOR
THE NEW YORK YANKEES

Batting Summary:	AB	R	H	2B	3B	HR	RBI	AVG.
Doyle	16	4	7	1	0	0	2	.438
Dent	24	3	10	1	0	0	7	.417
Jackson	23	2	9	1	0	2	8	.391
Blair	8	2	3	1	0	0	0	.375
White	24	9	8	0	0	1	4	.333
Rivers	18	2	6	0	0	0	1	.333
Munson	25	5	8	3	0	0	7	.320
Piniella	25	3	7	0	0	0	4	.280
Thomasson	4	0	1	0	0	0	0	.250
Stanley	5	0	1	1	0	0	0	.200
Chambliss	11	1	2	0	0	0	0	.182
Spencer	12	3	2	0	0	0	0	.167
Nettles	25	2	4	0	0	0	1	.160
Johnson	2	0	0	0	0	0	0	.000
Johnstone	0	0	0	0	0	0	0	.000
Heath	0	0	0	0	0	0	0	.000
TOTALS	222	36	68	8	0	3	34	.306

Pitching Summary:	G	IP	H	R	ER	BB	SO	ERA
Gossage (1-0)	3	6	1	0	0	1	4	0.00
Guidry (1-0)	1	9	8	1	1	7	4	1.00
Tidrow	2	4³/₃	4	1	1	0	5	1.93
Beattie (1-0)	1	9	9	2	2	4	8	2.00
Hunter (1-1)	2	13	13	6	6	1	5	4.17
Figueroa (0-1)	2	6²/₃	9	6	6	5	2	8.10
Clay	1	2¹/₃	4	4	3	2	2	11.61
Lindblad	1	2¹/₃	4	3	3	0	1	11.61
TOTALS	6	53	52	23	22	20	31	3.74

—SCORE BY INNINGS—

NEW YORK	1	4	6	3	0	4	13	4	0	1—36
LOS ANGELES	2	3	3	4	4	3	3	1	0	0—23

E — Dent 2, Lopes, Russell 3, Smith, Garvey, Ferguson. DP — New York 9, Los Angeles 4. LOB — New York 47, Los Angeles 38. SB — White 2, Piniella, North, Munson, Garvey, Rivers, Russell, Lopes 2. S — White, Davalillo. HBP — By Hooton (Jackson); by Forster (Jackson). WP — Clay, Hooton, Hough, Sutton. PB — Yeager and Oates.

Game One
Dodgers 11, Yankees 5

New York	AB	R	H	BI	Los Angeles	AB	R	H	BI
Rivers, CF	4	0	0	0	Lopes, 2B	5	2	2	5
Blair, CF	1	0	0	0	Russell, SS	5	1	3	0
White, LF	4	0	1	0	Smith, RF	5	0	1	1
Munson, C	4	1	0	0	Garvey, 1B	5	1	2	0
Jackson, DH	4	1	3	1	Cey, 3B	4	1	1	0
Piniella, LF	4	2	1	1	Baker, LF	4	2	3	1
Nettles, 3B	4	0	1	1	Monday, CF	2	2	1	0
Chambliss, 1B	4	1	1	0	North, CF	1	1	1	2
Stanley, 2B	2	0	1	0	Lacy, DH	3	0	1	1
Johnson, PH	1	0	0	0	Yeager, C	4	1	0	0
Doyle, 2B	0	0	0	0	John, P	0	0	0	0
Dent, SS	4	0	1	2	Forster, P	0	0	0	0
Figueroa, P	0	0	0	0					
Clay, P	0	0	0	0					
Lindblad, P	0	0	0	0					
Tidrow, P	0	0	0	0					
Totals	36	5	9	5	Totals	38	11	15	10

New York	000	000	320—5
Los Angeles	030	310	31x—11

E—Dent, Lopes, Russell. DP—New York 2, Los Angeles 1. LOB—New York 6, Los Angeles 6. 2B—Stanley, Monday, North, Russell. HR—Baker (1), Lopes (2), Jackson (1).

	IP	H	R	ER	BB	SO
Figueroa (L 0-1)	1 2-3	5	3	3	1	0
Clay	2 1-3	4	4	3	2	2
Lindblad	2 1-3	4	3	3	0	1
Tidrow	1 2-3	2	1	1	0	1
John (W 1-0)	7 2-3	8	5	3	2	4
Forster	1 1-3	1	0	0	0	3

WP—Clay. T—2:48. A—55,997.

Game Two
Dodgers 4, Yankees 3

New York	AB	R	H	BI	Los Angeles	AB	R	H	BI
White, LF	5	2	2	0	Lopes, 2B	4	1	1	0
Thompson, CF	3	0	1	0	Russell, SS	4	0	1	0
Blair, CF	1	0	1	0	Smith, RF	4	2	1	0
Munson, C	4	1	1	0	Garvey, 1B	3	0	1	0
Jackson, DH	4	0	1	3	Cey, 3B	3	1	2	4
Nettles, 3B	4	0	0	0	Baker, LF	3	0	0	0
Piniella, RF	4	0	2	0	Monday, CF	3	0	0	0
Spencer, 1B	4	0	1	0	North, CF	0	0	0	0
Doyle, 2B	3	0	1	0	Lacy, DH	3	0	0	0
Johnson, PH	1	0	0	0	Yeager, C	3	0	1	0
Stanley, 2B	0	0	0	0					
Dent, SS	4	0	1	0					
Totals	37	3	11	3	Totals	30	4	7	4

New York	002	000	100—3
Los Angeles	000	103	00x—4

DP—New York 1, Los Angeles 1. LOB—New York 10, Los Angeles 2. 2B—Munson, Jackson, Blair. HR—Cey (1). SB—White.

	IP	H	R	ER	BB	SO
Hunter (L 0-1)	6	7	4	4	0	2
Gossage	2	0	0	0	0	0
Hooton (W 1-0)	6	8	3	3	1	5
Forster	2 1-3	3	0	0	1	3
Welch	2-3	0	0	0	0	1

Save—Welch (1). HBP—Jackson (by Hooton). WP—Hooton. T—2:38. A—55,982.

Game Three
Yankees 5, Dodgers 1

Los Angeles	AB	R	H	BI	New York	AB	R	H	BI
Lopes, 2B	5	0	1	0	Rivers, CF	4	0	3	0
Russell, SS	4	0	2	1	Blair, CF	0	0	0	0
Smith, RF	4	0	1	0	White, LF	3	2	1	1
Garvey, 1B	4	0	1	0	Munson, C	4	1	1	1
Cey, 3B	3	0	0	0	Jackson, DH	3	0	1	1
Baker, LF	3	0	2	0	Piniella, RF	4	0	1	1
Lacy, DH	4	0	1	0	Nettles, 3B	4	1	1	0
North, CF	3	1	0	0	Chambliss, 1B	3	0	1	0
Yeager, C	1	0	0	0	Doyle, 2B	4	0	0	0
Mota, PH	0	0	0	0	Dent, SS	4	1	1	1
Grote, C	0	0	0	0	Guidry, P	0	0	0	0
Ferguson, C	1	0	0	0					
Sutton, P	0	0	0	0					
Rautzhn, P	0	0	0	0					
Hough, P	0	0	0	0					
Totals	32	1	8	1	Totals	33	5	10	5

Los Angeles	001	000	000—1
New York	110	000	30x—5

E—Dent. DP—New York 2. LOB—Los Angeles 11, New York 7. 2B—Garvey. HR—White (1). SB—North, Piniella.

	IP	H	R	ER	BB	SO
Sutton (L 0-1)	6 1-3	9	5	5	3	2
Rautzhan	2-3	1	0	0	0	0
Hough	1	0	0	0	0	0
Guidry (W 1-0)	9	8	1	1	7	4

T—2:27. A—56,447.

Game Four
Yankees 4, Dodgers 3

Los Angeles	AB	R	H	BI	New York	AB	R	H	BI
Lopes, 2B	4	1	0	0	Blair, CF	4	1	2	0
Russell, SS	5	0	2	0	Rivers, PH	1	0	0	0
Smith, RF	4	1	1	3	White, LF	3	2	1	0
Garvey, 1B	4	0	0	0	Munson, C	3	1	2	1
Cey, 3B	4	0	1	0	Jackson, DH	4	0	2	1
Baker, LF	4	0	0	0	Piniella, RF	5	0	1	1
Monday, DH	2	0	1	0	Nettles, 3B	4	0	0	0
North, CF	4	0	0	0	Chambliss, 1B	4	0	0	0
Yeager, C	3	1	1	0	Stanley, 2B	3	0	0	0
Davilillo, PH	1	0	0	0					
Spencer, PH	1	0	0	0					
Grote, C	0	0	0	0					
Grote, C	0	0	0	0	Doyle, 2B	0	0	0	0
					Dent, SS	4	0	1	0
Total	35	3	6	3	Total	36	4	9	3

Los Angeles		000	030	000		0—3	
New York		000	002	010		1—4	

Two out when winning run scored.

E—Russell. DP—New York 1. LOB—Los Angeles 7, New York 8. 2B—Yeager, Munson. HR—Smith (1). SB—Garvey, Munson. S—White.

	IP	H	R	ER	BB	SO
John	7	6	3	2	2	2
Forster	1-3	1	0	0	0	0
Welch (L 0-1)	2 1-3	2	1	1	1	3
Figueroa	5	4	3	3	4	2
Tidrow	3	2	0	0	0	4
Gossage (W 1-0)	2	0	0	0	1	2

HBP—Jackson (by Forster). T—3:17. A—56,445.

Game Five
Yankees 12, Dodgers 2

Los Angeles	AB	R	H	BI	New York	AB	R	H	BI
Lopes, 2B	4	2	2	0	Rivers, CF	5	2	3	1
Russell, SS	5	0	2	1	Blair, CF	1	1	0	0
Smith, RF	4	0	1	1	White, LF	5	2	2	3
Garvey, 1B	4	0	1	0	Johnston, RF	0	0	0	0
Cey, 3B	3	0	1	0	Munson, C	5	1	3	5
Baker, LF	4	0	0	0	Heath, C	0	0	0	0
Monday, CF	3	0	0	0	Jackson, DH	3	0	1	0
Lacy, DH	4	0	0	0	Piniella, RF	4	0	1	1
Yeager, C	2	0	1	0	Thompson, LF	1	0	0	0
Oates, C	1	0	1	0	Nettles, 3B	5	0	1	0
					Spencer, 1B	4	2	1	0
					Doyle, 2B	5	2	3	0
					Dent, SS	4	2	3	1
Total	34	2	9	2	Total	42	12	18	11

Los Angeles		101	000	000 —2	
New York		004	300	41x—12	

E—Russell, Smith, Garvey. DP—Los Angeles 2, New York 1. LOB—Los Angeles 9, New York 10. 2B—Russell, Munson, Dent. SB—Lopes, Rivers, White, Russell.

	IP	H	R	ER	BB	SO
Hooton (L 1-1)	2 1-3	5	4	3	2	1
Rautzhan	1 1-3	3	3	3	0	0
Hough	4 1-3	10				
Hough	4 1-3	10	5	5	2	5
Beattie (W 1-0)	9	9	2	2	4	8

WP—Hough. PB—Yeager 2. T—2:56. A—56,448.

Game Six
Yankees 7, Dodgers 2

New York	AB	R	H	BI	Los Angeles	AB	R	H	BI
Rivers, CF	4	0	0	0	Lopes, 2B	4	1	2	2
Blair, CF	1	0	0	0	Russell, SS	3	0	1	0
White, LF	4	1	1	0	Smith, RF	4	0	0	0
Thompson, LF	0	0	0	0	Garvey, 1B	4	0	0	0
Munson, C	5	0	1	0	Cey, 3B	4	0	1	0
Jackson, DH	5	1	1	2	Baker, LF	3	0	0	0
Piniella, RF	4	1	1	0	Monday, CF	3	0	0	0
Johnston, RF	0	0	0	0	Ferguson, C	3	1	2	0
Nettles, 3B	4	1	1	0	Davilillo, DH	2	0	1	0
Spencer, 1B	3	1	0	0					
Doyle, 2B	4	2	3	2					
Dent, SS	4	0	3	3					
Total	38	7	11	7	Total	30	2	7	2

New York		030	002	200—7	
Los Angeles		101	000	000—2	

E—Ferguson, DP—New York 2. LOB—New York 6, Los Angeles 3. 2B—Ferguson 2, Doyle. HR—Lopes (3), Jackson (2). SB—Lopes. S—Davalillo.

	IP	H	R	ER	BB	SO
Hunter (W 1-1)	7	6	2	2	1	3
Gossage	2	1	0	0	0	2
Sutton (L 0-2)	5 2-3	8	5	5	1	6
Welch	1 1-3	2	2	2	1	2
Rau	2	1	0	0	0	3

WP—Sutton. T—2:34. A—55,985.

Index